200 chicken

D1045619

200 chicken dishes

hamlyn **all color**

Sara Lewis

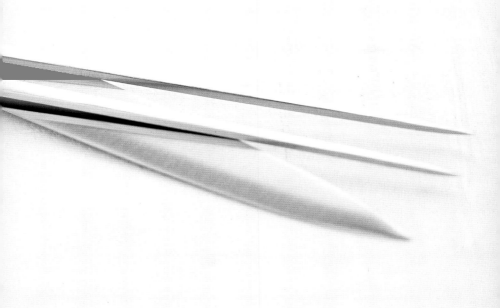

For Alice, who enthusiastically ate her way through all the
recipes and who will, I hope, try cooking them too!

An Hachette UK Company
www.hachette.co.uk

First published in Great Britain in 2009 by Hamlyn,
a division of Octopus Publishing Group Ltd,
2–4 Heron Quays, London E14 4JP
www.octopusbooksusa.com

Distributed in the U.S. and Canada by Octopus Books USA:
c/o Hachette Book Group USA
237 Park Avenue
New York NY 10017

Some of the recipes in this book have previously
appeared in other books published by Hamlyn.

ISBN: 978-0-600-61945-1

A CIP catalog record for this book is available from the
Library of Congress

Printed and bound in China

2 3 4 5 6 7 8 9 10

Standard level spoon measures are used in all recipes.

Ovens should be preheated to the specified temperature.
If using a fan-assisted oven, follow the manufacturer's
instructions for adjusting the time and temperature.

Poultry should be cooked thoroughly. To test if poultry
is cooked, pierce the flesh through the thickest part with
a skewer or fork—the juices should run clear, never
pink or red.

People with known nut allergies should avoid recipes
containing nuts or nut derivatives, and vulnerable people
should avoid dishes containing raw or lightly cooked eggs.

contents

introduction   6

light lunches   18

easy suppers   70

food for friends   144

favorite roasts   196

two meals from one   216

index   236

acknowledgments   240

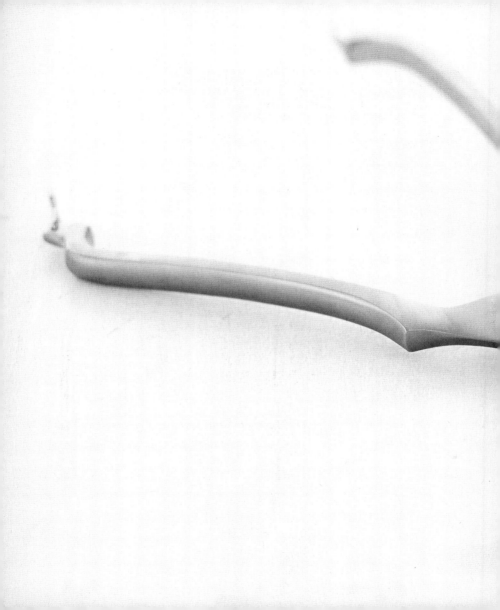

introduction

introduction

As you push your cart around the supermarket for your weekly food shop, you will probably add one or two packs of chicken, perhaps a pack of boneless, skinless breasts, some thighs or a whole chicken, not forgetting mini breast fillets, ground chicken, chicken livers, or drumsticks. The different cuts cover a wide range of prices, so there is something for every budget. But it is all too easy to go into "automatic pilot," as we juggle hectic workloads, family commitments, and daily chores, and just cook the same old recipes. Chicken is highly versatile, and with 200 recipes to choose from in this book we hope that you will be able to add some new favorites to your family's repertoire.

Much has been made in the media about the welfare of chickens during rearing. For those on a tight budget, battery-farmed chickens may be the only option. Try to use up the leftovers the following day, or use the redundant carcass to make stock, so that a more expensive free-range chicken, even if not organic, is more cost-effective. While organic, free-range chickens may not be for everyone, try to choose whole chickens and chicken joints with labels indicating that the birds have been reared humanely (for more information, consult the RSPCA in the UK or the HSUS in the USA).

The recipes in this book have been grouped into chapters so that you can quickly

find one to suit your needs, whether it be for a light snack, some party food, or a full evening meal. When you are really short of time you can choose from Gingered Chicken with Soft Noodles (see page 20), Seared Chicken & Vegetable Wraps (see page 56), or Peppered Chicken & Eggplants (see page 140), all ready including preparation and cooking within 30 minutes. For an easy midweek supper what about chillied Chicken Arrabiata (see page 84), Blackened Chicken & Beans (see page 116), or Thai Sesame Chicken Patties (see page 118)? For something a little more traditional there are Chicken, Bacon, & Sage Meatballs (see page 130) or Chicken Thatch (see page 132), the poultry version of Shepherds Pie.

If it suits you better then opt for a supper that requires little preparation but that can then be left in the oven to cook slowly, leaving you free to get on with something else. Chicken Stew & Dumplings (see page 96), packed with root vegetables and pearl barley simmered with pale ale or Stoved Chicken with Black Pudding (see page 120), a Scottish inspired casserole topped with sliced potatoes would fit the bill perfectly.

For a meal to share with friends why not try Chicken Mole (see page 154), a Mexican dish with chocolate, or Chicken & Mushroom Lasagna (see page 164). Both can be made up earlier in the day then reheated when needed. For something to impress what about Baked Chicken in a Salt Crust with red pepper ketchup (see page 172) or Italian Chicken Cushion (see page 184), a boned whole chicken stuffed with a delicious mix of basil, sundried tomatoes, and olives. For a more leisurely relaxing Sunday lunch choose one of the comforting roasts with a twist, perfect for all seasons with an option for dinner for two.

There's a whole chapter on what to do with the leftovers, from Chicken & Spinach Chowder (see page 218) to Chicken & Avocado Salad (see page 228) or Cheesy Chicken & Chutney Puffs (see page 230) that make maximum use of the leftover bits from a roast along with tips on making stock so that nothing is wasted.

Influenced by a fusion of flavors from around the world, from Thailand to the Caribbean, plain chicken will be a thing of the past. So, if you are in need of inspiration to awaken those taste buds, read on.

Hygiene essentials

- Keep raw and cooked chicken separate in the refrigerator so that raw chicken juices cannot drip onto other foods.
- Cover food dishes so that chicken does not dry out.
- Use separate boards and knives for preparing raw and cooked chicken, as well as for preparing meat and vegetables.
- Defrost frozen chicken in the refrigerator, transferring to room temperature for 1–2 hours before cooking.
- Only reheat cooked food once, and make sure it is piping hot all the way through. Don't warm foods, especially if using the microwave.
- Raw chicken that has been defrosted can only be put back in the freezer if it has been cooked and cooled. If taken out of the freezer in a cooked state, it cannot be refrozen.
- Add a small frozen ice pack to lunchboxes, and use an insulated lunchbag so that any cooked chicken stays cold.

How to make chicken stock

Why bother making your own stock? In an age when we are all being advised to cut down on our salt consumption, homemade stock can be salt-free; it also fits in with our general tendency to recycle all we can. If you haven't got time to make stock now, don't throw the chicken carcass out—just pack it into a plastic bag and freeze it until you do have time. The following recipe makes about 6 cups.

chicken carcass from a roast or poached
   whole bird
8 cups **cold water**
1 large **onion**, cut into quarters but still with
   the inner brown layer of skin attached
2 **carrots**, thickly sliced
2 **celery sticks**, thickly sliced
small bunch of **mixed fresh herbs** or a **dried
   bouquet garni**
black peppercorns

Put the chicken carcass into a large saucepan with the measured water, and add the onion, carrots, and celery. Flavor with the fresh herbs or bouquet garni and a few black peppercorns, then bring to a boil. Partially cover the top of the pan with a lid, then allow to simmer gently for 2 hours. Strain into a pitcher and allow to cool. Store in the refrigerator for 2–3 days or freeze in handy-sized plastic containers or well-sealed plastic bags if the carcass had not already been frozen.

Preparation

Before use, always rinse chicken well in cold water, drain well, and pat dry with paper towels; this is especially important if you are using prepacked raw chicken. When rinsing a whole chicken, take extra care to rinse inside the bird, and remove giblets if included.

If using frozen chicken, make sure it is completely defrosted before use. Don't try to speed up defrosting by plunging it into warm water. Immerse in cold water and change the water frequently, or defrost in the microwave, following the manufacturer's guidelines.

Is the chicken cooked?

Chicken must never be served rare or medium, but always well done. Insert a skewer or small knife into the thickest part of a joint, or through a thigh to the breast if cooking a whole chicken. The juices will run clear when the chicken is ready—if you see any traces of pink in the juices, continue cooking. If pan-frying or broiling, check at 5-minute intervals. For a whole chicken, retest after 15 minutes more in the oven.

How to joint a whole chicken

This is not as tricky as it may first seem; the secret is to have a good sharp knife and locate the joints by feel before cutting through them to separate. This technique can be adapted to cut up guineafowl, turkey, duck, or other poultry.

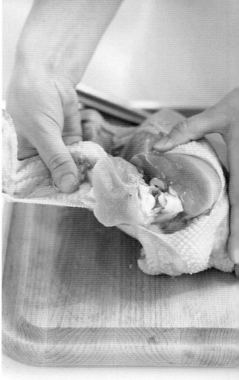

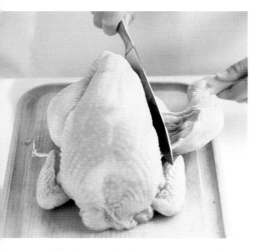

1 First remove the trussing strings and put the chicken breast side uppermost on a cutting board. Pull one leg gently away from the body. Cut through the skin between the body and leg, cut down through the meat, and then work down to the thigh joint. Bend the leg so that it eases the leg bone from its socket, then cut through the ball-and-socket joint. Repeat with the other leg.

2 To remove the wings, press one wing against the body of the bird so that both parts of the shoulder are visible. Cut through the skin, then down through the joint to sever. Tuck the wingtip under the shoulder to make a triangular shape joint. Repeat with the other wing.

3 Split the carcass by cutting around and under both breasts with poultry shears or strong kitchen scissors. Cut through the rib cage, so separating the backbone from the breasts. Repeat on the other side.

4 Cut along the center of the breast with poultry shears, strong kitchen scissors, or a sharp knife, then either slide a knife under the breast meat on each side of the bone to release two boneless breast joints or cut straight down between the breast bone with a large cook's knife to give two joints on the bone. For a "supreme" leave the wing joint attached at step 2, but sever at the first joint so separating wing tips from body.

5 Now separate the leg joint into a drumstick and thigh. Put the joint skin side uppermost, then flex the drumstick slightly so that you can see where the central joint is. Cut through the ball-and-socket joint. Repeat with the other leg.

6 You should now have 2 drumsticks, 2 thigh joints, 2 wings, and 2 breast joints, plus a carcass (not pictured) to make stock with. When the bird is small, leave the drumstick and thigh joint joined together.

How to spatchcock a chicken or poussin

Here the bird is split and then flattened so that it cooks more quickly. This enables a whole bird to be grilled, broiled, or roasted traditionally in a shorter time.

1 Put the chicken or poussin breast side down on a cutting board and remove the trussing string. Cut the bird in half using poultry shears or sturdy kitchen scissors.

2 Turn the bird over, then using the palm of your hand press down on the breast and flatten it slightly.

3 Trim off the knuckle bones from the drumsticks and tuck the wingtips under the bird. Neaten off any untidy skin and insert two long metal or wooden skewers through each leg, breast, and wing so that they cross under the bird and keep it flat during roasting or grilling.

How to carve a roast chicken

A good carving knife and fork are essential. Choose a knife that has a long, slightly flexible blade and a fork with tines that are close together. Even more importantly, you must keep the knife sharp. If you find using a knife steel too daunting, there are many hand or electrical knife sharpeners available from good cookstores or major department stores—it really is worth investing in one. Carve off just the amounts you need at a time, working first on one side and then on the other side of the bird, as needed. If the bird is stuffed, don't forget to serve the stuffing with a spoon.

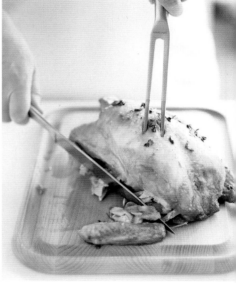

1 Put the chicken on a large cutting board or serving plate with the breast side uppermost. Steadying the joint with a carving fork, cut the skin between the breast and one thigh joint and work downward through the meat to the joint. Bend the leg outward to locate the thigh joint, then cut down through the joint to remove the first leg.

2 To remove the wing on the same side of the chicken, cut down through the corner of the breast to the wing joint. Flex the wing as you did for the leg to locate the joint, then cut down between the joint to remove the wing.

3 Working on the same side of the chicken, make thin diagonal cuts down the breast to slice the meat, using the fork to steady the joint and to help you to remove each slice.

4 Now that the breast has been sliced, separate the thigh and drumstick joints, then cut thin slices of meat off both joints that follow the direction of the bone.

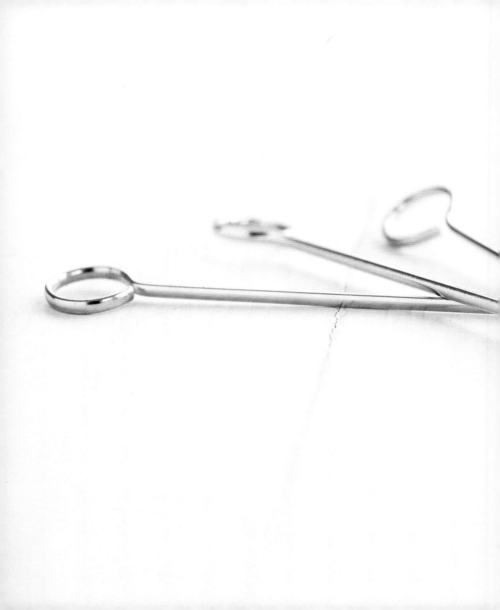

light
lunches

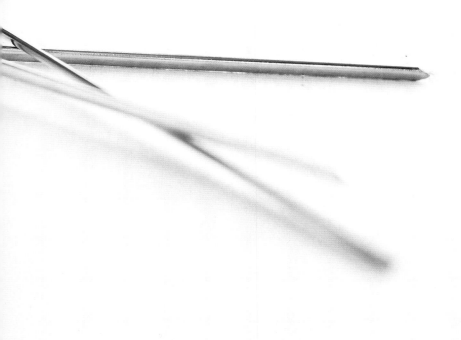

gingered chicken with soft noodles

Serves **4**
Preparation time **10 minutes**
Cooking time **12–13 minutes**

2 teaspoons **sesame oil**
2 teaspoons **sunflower oil**
2 boneless, skinless **chicken breasts**, diced
1 inch piece **ginger root**, peeled, finely grated
10 oz pack **ready-prepared stir-fry crunchy vegetables**
¼ cup **ready-salted peanuts**, roughly chopped
13 oz **chilled fresh egg noodles**
2 tablespoons **sweet chili dipping sauce**
3 tablespoons **soy sauce**
2 teaspoons **fish sauce** (optional)
small bunch **cilantro**, to garnish (optional)

Pour the oils into a wok or large skillet. When hot, add the chicken and stir-fry for 5 minutes, until lightly browned. Add the garlic and ginger and cook for 1 minute.

Add the mixed vegetables and stir-fry for 3 minutes. Mix in the peanuts and the noodles and stir-fry for 2–3 minutes until hot. Add the chili sauce, soy sauce, and fish sauce, if using, and cook for 1 minute. Spoon into small bowls, and garnish with torn cilantro leaves, if desired.

For gingered chicken with bean sprout salad, fry the chicken as above, omitting the stir-fried vegetables and noodles, then allow to cool. Mix 2 cups rinsed bean sprouts with 1 finely shredded romaine lettuce, 1 carrot, and 1 zucchini, both coarsely grated. Add the chicken, peanuts, and sauces and toss together. Garnish with torn cilantro.

seared chicken sandwich

Serves **4**
Preparation time **15 minutes**
Cooking time **5–6 minutes**

8 oz **mini chicken breast fillets**
8 teaspoons **balsamic vinegar**
8 slices **multigrain bread**
6 tablespoons **low-fat plain yogurt**
½–1 teaspoon **freshly grated hot horseradish** or **horseradish sauce**, to taste
2 cups **mixed salad leaves with beet strips**
pepper

Put the mini chicken breast fillets into a plastic bag with half the vinegar and toss together until evenly coated.

Heat a nonstick skillet, lift the chicken out of the plastic bag with a fork and add the pieces to the pan. Fry for 3 minutes, turn and drizzle with the vinegar from the bag, and cook for 2–3 more minutes or until browned and cooked through.

Toast the bread lightly on both sides. Slice the chicken into long, thin strips and arrange them on 4 slices of toast. Mix together the yogurt and horseradish and a little pepper to taste. Add the salad leaves and toss together.

Spoon the yogurt and salad leaves over the chicken, drizzle over the remaining vinegar, if desired, and top with the remaining slices of toast. Cut each sandwich in half and serve immediately.

For tangy chicken, lemon, and garlic toasties,

toss the chicken fillets with the juice of ½ lemon and 1 tablespoon olive oil then fry as above but without the vinegar. Toast 8 slices whole-wheat bread then spread with 4 tablespoons garlic mayonnaise. Divide the chicken between 4 slices of toast then top with the shredded leaves of 2 small crisphead lettuces and a 2 inch piece cucumber, thinly sliced. Cover with the remaining slices of toast then press together and cut into triangles.

quinoa salad with seared chicken

Serves **4**
Preparation time **25 minutes**
Cooking time **22 minutes**

¾ cup **quinoa**
¼ **cucumber**, finely diced
1 small **green bell pepper**,
  cored, seeded, finely diced
6 **scallions**, trimmed, thinly
  sliced
⅔ cup **frozen peas**,
  just defrosted
grated zest and juice of
  1 **lemon**
2 tablespoons **olive oil**
1 tablespoon **harissa paste**
4 boneless, skinless **chicken
  breasts**, cut into long
  thin slices
small bunch **mint**, finely
  chopped

For the dressing
3 tablespoons **olive oil**
1 tablespoon **harissa paste**
grated zest and juice of
  1 **lemon**
salt

Add the quinoa to a saucepan of boiling water and simmer for about 10 minutes or according to package instructions until just tender, then drain in a fine sieve.

Make the dressing by mixing the olive oil, harissa, lemon zest and juice, and a little salt in a salad bowl. Stir in the hot quinoa and allow to cool, then mix in the cucumber, green pepper, scallions, and frozen peas.

Mix the lemon zest and juice, oil, and harissa in a shallow bowl, then add the chicken and toss well. Heat a griddle pan (or ordinary skillet), then cook the chicken in batches for about 6 minutes, turning until browned on both sides and cooked through.

Stir the mint through the quinoa salad, then top with the warm chicken. Serve warm or cold. Any leftovers can be chilled and packed into lunchboxes the following day.

For hot feta & almond quinoa with seared chicken, toss the just-cooked quinoa in the dressing as above. Omit the cucumber, adding 1 seeded and chopped red bell pepper instead, and ⅓ cup golden raisins and ½ cup ready-to-eat dried apricots, diced, in place of the peas. Sprinkle with 4 oz drained and crumbled feta cheese and ½ cup toasted slivered almonds. Top with the chicken and serve hot with extra spoonfuls of harissa.

asian citrus chicken skewers

Serves **4**

Preparation time **5 minutes**, plus marinating

Cooking time **20 minutes**

1 lb boneless, skinless **chicken breasts**, cubed

grated zest and juice of 1 **lemon**

2 teaspoons **Chinese 5-spice powder**

1 tablespoon **dark soy sauce**

mixed vegetables (carrots, scallions, radishes), cut into strips, to serve (optional)

Place the chicken, lemon zest and juice, 5-spice powder, and soy sauce in a bowl. Stir to combine, cover, then allow to marinate in the refrigerator for at least 1 hour or overnight.

Thread the chicken pieces onto 4 presoaked wooden skewers, pushing them tightly together. Broil for 10 minutes under a preheated moderate broiler. Turn the skewers, baste with any remaining marinade, and broil for an additional 10 minutes. Serve on a bed of vegetables, if desired.

For piri piri chicken skewers, mix the grated lemon zest and juice with 2 tablespoons olive oil then add 2 teaspoons piri piri seasoning, 2 teaspoons tomato paste, and 2 finely chopped garlic cloves. Add the chicken, marinate, then broil as above.

teriyaki chicken with three seeds

Serves **4**

Preparation time **20 minutes**,
plus marinating

Cooking time **16–20 minutes**

4 boneless, skinless **chicken
breasts**, about 4 oz each

2 tablespoons **sunflower oil**

4 tablespoons **soy sauce**

2 **garlic cloves**, finely
chopped

1 inch piece **ginger root**,
finely grated

2 tablespoons **sesame seeds**

2 tablespoons **sunflower
seeds**

2 tablespoons **pumpkin
seeds**

juice of 2 **limes**

2 cups **herb salad**

½ small **iceberg lettuce**,
torn into bite-size pieces

1½ cups **alfalfa** or **brocco
sprouting seeds**

Put the chicken breasts into a shallow china dish.
Spoon three-quarters of the oil over the chicken, then
add half the soy sauce, the garlic, and the ginger. Turn
the chicken to coat in the mixture, then allow to
marinate for 30 minutes.

Heat a nonstick skillet, then lift the chicken out of the
marinade and add to the pan. Fry for 8–10 minutes
each side until dark brown and cooked all the way
through. Lift out and set aside.

Heat the remaining oil in the pan, add the seeds
and fry for 2–3 minutes until lightly toasted. Add the
remaining marinade and remaining soy sauce, bring to
a boil, then take off the heat and mix in the lime juice.

Mix the herb salad, lettuce, and sprouting seeds
together, then spoon over 4 serving plates. Thinly slice
the chicken and arrange on top, then spoon the seed
and lime dressing over the top. Serve at once.

For teriyaki chicken with Asian salad, marinate the
chicken as above and make a salad with 7 oz carrots,
cut into thin strips, 4 scallions, cut into thin strips,
6 thinly sliced radishes, and ½ small head of Chinese
cabbage, thinly shredded. Fry the chicken as above,
omit the seeds, and then continue with the dressing
as above. Slice the chicken, arrange on the salad, and
drizzle with the warm dressing.

chicken with sweet potato wedges

Serves **4**
Preparation time **20 minutes**
Cooking time **35 minutes**

4 **sweet potatoes**, about
  2½ lb in total, scrubbed
4 **chicken thighs**, boned,
  skinned, cut into chunks
1 **red onion**, cut into wedges
4 **plum tomatoes**, cut into
  chunks
5 oz **chorizo** in one piece,
  skinned, sliced or diced
  depending on diameter
3 stems **rosemary**, leaves
  torn from stems
4 tablespoons **olive oil**
salt and **pepper**

Cut the potatoes in half, then into thick wedges, and put them into a large roasting pan with the chicken, onion, and tomatoes. Tuck the chorizo in and around the potatoes, then sprinkle with the rosemary and some salt and pepper.

Drizzle with the oil, then roast in a preheated oven, 400°F, for about 35 minutes, turning once or twice until the chicken is golden and cooked through and the potato wedges browned and tender.

Spoon onto serving plates and serve as it is, or with a watercress salad.

For mixed roots with fennel & chicken, use 2½ lb of mixed baking potatoes, parsnips, and carrots. Peel the parsnips, and carrots, then cut all vegetables into wedges. Add to the roasting pan with the chicken as above. Sprinkle with 2 teaspoons fennel seeds, 1 teaspoon turmeric, and 1 teaspoon paprika, then drizzle with 4 tablespoons olive oil and roast as above.

spiced chicken & mango salad

Serves **4**
Preparation time **15 minutes**
Cooking time **5–6 minutes**

4 small boneless, skinless
  chicken breasts
6 teaspoons **mild curry paste**
Juice of 1 **lemon**
1 cup **low-fat plain yogurt**
1 **mango**
1¼ cups **watercress**
½ **cucumber**, diced
½ **red onion**, chopped
½ **iceberg lettuce**

Cut the chicken breasts into long, thin slices. Put 4 teaspoons of the curry paste in a plastic bag with the lemon juice and mix together by squeezing the bag. Add the chicken and toss together.

Half-fill the base of a steamer with water and bring to a boil. Place the chicken in the top of the steamer in a single layer, cover and steam for 5–6 minutes until thoroughly cooked. Test the chicken (see page 11).

Meanwhile, mix the remaining curry paste in a bowl with the yogurt.

Cut a thick slice off either side of the mango to reveal the large, flat pit. Trim the flesh away from the pit, then remove the peel and cut the flesh into bite-size chunks.

Rinse the watercress with cold water and tear it into bite-size pieces. Add to the yogurt dressing with the cucumber, red onion, and mango and toss gently.

Tear the lettuce into pieces, divide it among 4 plates, spoon the mango mixture on top and complete with the warm chicken strips.

For coronation chicken, mix the curry paste and yogurt with 4 tablespoons mayonnaise. Stir in 1 lb cold cooked diced chicken and ¼ cup golden raisins. Sprinkle with ¼ cup toasted slivered almonds and serve on a bed of mixed salad and herb leaves.

chicken liver pâté with mushrooms

Serves **4**
Preparation time **25 minutes**,
  plus chilling
Cooking time **20 minutes**

⅓ cup **dried porcini
  mushrooms**
¾ cup **boiling water**
2 tablespoons **butter**
1 tablespoon **olive oil**
1 **red onion**, roughly chopped
7½ oz pack **frozen chicken
  livers**, defrosted
2 **garlic cloves**, finely
  chopped
2–3 stems **thyme**, leaves
  torn from stems
6 tablespoons **red wine**
salt and **pepper**

For the butter layer
½ **red onion**, thinly sliced
thyme leaves
⅓ cup **butter**

Soak the dried mushrooms in a heatproof bowl just covered with the boiling water for 15 minutes. Meanwhile, heat the butter and oil in a skillet, add the onion, and fry gently for 10 minutes until softened and just beginning to brown.

Tip the chicken livers into a sieve, rinse with cold water, drain well, then roughly chop, discarding any white cores. Add to the onions with the garlic and fry for 4–5 minutes, stirring until browned.

Add the mushrooms and their soaking liquid, the thyme leaves, red wine, and some seasoning. Cover and cook for 5 minutes, then cool slightly.

Puree the liver mixture in a food processor or blender until smooth. Spoon into four small dishes and level the surface.

Sprinkle the raw onion and thyme leaves over the pâté. Melt the butter in a small saucepan, tilt the pan and scoop the clear melted butter onto the pâté, discarding the cloudy white milk solids in the bottom of the pan. Cover and chill for 3–4 hours or overnight until firm. Serve with toast and arugula leaves.

For brandied chicken liver & pistachio pâté, omit the mushrooms. Add 2 tablespoons brandy to the fried chicken livers and, when bubbling, flame with a taper. Omit the red wine and add ⅔ cup chicken stock (see page 10) along with the thyme leaves. Puree, then mix in ½ cup sliced pistachios, saving a few for the buttery top layer.

thai red chicken & cashew sauce

Serves **2**
Preparation time **8 minutes**
Cooking time **9–12 minutes**

10 oz boneless **chicken
thighs**, thickly sliced
5 tablespoons **Thai red
curry paste**
2 **pita breads**, split in half
horizontally

For the cashew sauce
1¼ cups **cashew nuts**, lightly
toasted
1 teaspoon **dried red pepper
flakes**
3 tablespoons **soy sauce**
1 cup **coconut milk**
3 tablespoons **cilantro leaves**,
plus extra to garnish
2 tablespoons **palm sugar** or
light brown sugar
2 tablespoons **rice wine
vinegar**
2 **kaffir lime leaves**,
shredded

To make the cashew sauce, place the nuts in a food
processor and pulse until finely chopped. Place in a
small pan with the remaining sauce ingredients and
heat gently for 4–5 minutes, stirring frequently to
prevent sticking, until the sauce is thick and glossy.

Mix the chicken slices with the red curry paste and
thread onto 4 metal skewers.

Preheat a sandwich grill and lay the skewers directly
on the heat, bringing down the top plate to seal the
chicken. Grill for 5–6 minutes, until the chicken is
thoroughly cooked. Remove from the heat and set aside.

When the meat is cool enough to handle, push the
chicken off the skewers directly into the pita breads.
Toast the breads in the cleaned sandwich grill for
1–2 minutes, or according to the manufacturer's
instructions, until they are crispy and the chicken hot.

Cut each pita in half, garnish with cilantro leaves,
and serve immediately with a bowl of the warm
cashew sauce.

For Thai red chicken with lime-dressed zucchini,
cook the chicken on skewers as above. While the
chicken cools slightly, mix 1 tablespoon sunflower oil
with the grated zest and juice of 1 lime, 2 tablespoons
roughly chopped cilantro, and seasoning in a plastic
bag. Add 2 zucchini, cut into thin lengthwise slices,
and toss in the bag. Lift out with a fork and add to
the sandwich grill, then cook until lightly browned.
Arrange on plates, drizzle with the remaining dressing,
and top with the chicken. Serve with rice.

griddled chicken & fennel pockets

Serves **4**

Preparation time **15 minutes**

Cooking time **9–10 minutes**

14 oz **mini chicken breast fillets**, thinly sliced

1 **fennel bulb**, thinly sliced

2 tablespoons **olive oil**

2 **garlic cloves**, finely chopped

4 **pita breads**

2 **oranges**, peeled, cut into segments

1 cup **watercress**

salt and **pepper**

For the dressing

2 tablespoons **low-fat plain yogurt**

1 teaspoon **wholegrain mustard**

1 teaspoon **honey**

salt and **pepper**

Toss the chicken and fennel with the oil, garlic, and a little seasoning. Preheat a griddle pan (or ordinary skillet), then add the pita breads and cook for 1–2 minutes, turning until hot and puffy. Remove from the pan and keep hot.

Add the chicken and fennel to the pan and fry for about 8 minutes, turning once until browned and cooked through. Meanwhile, make the dressing by mixing the yogurt with the mustard, honey, and a little seasoning.

Slit the pita breads and fill with the orange segments, watercress, chicken, and fennel, then drizzle the dressing over and serve immediately.

For chicken pitas with carrot salad, fry the chicken with oil and garlic as above but omit the fennel. Mix 2 tablespoons olive oil with 2 teaspoons wholegrain mustard, the juice of ½ orange, and seasoning, then stir in 2 grated carrots, 2 tablespoons golden raisins, and a small handful of torn cilantro. Divide between warmed pitas and add the chicken.

deviled chicken

Serves **4**
Preparation time **10 minutes**
Cooking time **16–20 minutes**

8 boneless **chicken thighs**
salad leaves, to serve

For the devil sauce
2 tablespoons **Dijon mustard**
6 drops **Tabasco sauce**
2 **garlic cloves**, crushed
1 tablespoon **soy sauce**

Heat a large griddle pan (or ordinary skillet). Remove the skin from the chicken thighs, open them out, and trim away any fat.

To make the devil sauce, mix together the mustard, Tabasco, garlic, and soy sauce in a shallow dish.

Dip the trimmed chicken thighs in the devil sauce and coat each piece well. Place the chicken pieces flat on the pan and cook for 8–10 minutes on each side.

Serve hot or cold with salad leaves.

For jerk chicken, mix 3 tablespoons jerk marinade (a ready-made paste) with the grated zest and juice of ½ an orange and 2 finely chopped garlic cloves. Dip the chicken in this mixture then cook as above. Serve with rice or a salad.

warm chicken salad with anchovies

Serves **4**
Preparation time **20 minutes**
Cooking time **11–14 minutes**

5 oz **green beans**, thickly
   sliced
1 small **crisp lettuce**, leaves
   separated and torn into
   pieces
6 **scallions**, thinly sliced
6 oz **cherry tomatoes**, halved
9 oz jar **mixed pepper
   antipasto in oil**
2 boneless, skinless **chicken
   breasts**, diced
1 cup **fresh bread crumbs**
4 canned **anchovy fillets**,
   drained, chopped

For the dressing
3 tablespoons **olive oil**
2 teaspoons **sundried
   tomato paste**
4 teaspoons **red wine vinegar**
salt and **pepper**

Blanch the green beans in a saucepan of boiling water for 3–4 minutes until just tender. Drain, rinse with cold water, and drain again.

Put the beans, lettuce, scallions, and tomatoes into a large salad bowl. Lift the peppers out of the jar, reserving the oil, dice if needed and add to the salad.

Pour 2 tablespoons oil from the pepper jar into a skillet, add the chicken and fry for 8–10 minutes, stirring until golden and cooked through. Spoon over the salad. Heat 1 tablespoon extra oil in the pan, add the bread crumbs and anchovies, and stir-fry until golden.

Mix the dressing ingredients together, toss over the salad, then sprinkle with the breadcrumbs and anchovies and serve immediately.

For chicken Caesar salad, mix the green beans with 4 hard-cooked eggs cut into wedges, scallions, and lettuce as above, plus 4 chopped anchovy fillets. Cut 3 oz bread into cubes and fry in 2 tablespoons olive oil and 2 tablespoons butter. Mix 4 tablespoons mayonnaise with 1 finely chopped garlic clove and the juice of 1 lime. Toss with the salad, then sprinkle with croutons and ½ cup grated Parmesan cheese.

griddled summer chicken salad

Serves **4**
Preparation time **15 minutes**
Cooking time **45 minutes**

4 x 4 oz boneless, skinless
  chicken breasts
2 small **red onions**
2 **red bell peppers**, cored,
  seeded, cut into flat pieces
1 bunch **asparagus**, trimmed
7 oz **new potatoes**, boiled,
  cut in half
1 bunch **basil**
5 tablespoons **olive oil**
2 tablespoons **balsamic**
  vinegar
salt and **pepper**

Heat a griddle pan (or ordinary skillet). Place the chicken breasts in the pan and cook for 8–10 minutes on each side. When cooked, remove from the pan and cut roughly into chunks.

Cut the red onions into wedges, keeping the root ends intact to hold the wedges together. Place in the pan and cook for 5 minutes on each side. Remove from the pan and set aside.

Place the flat pieces of red pepper in the pan and cook for 8 minutes on the skin side only, so that the skins are charred and blistered. Remove and set aside, then cook the asparagus in the pan for 6 minutes, turning frequently.

Put the boiled potatoes in a large bowl. Tear the basil, reserving a few leaves intact to garnish, and add to the bowl, together with the chicken and all the vegetables. Add the olive oil, balsamic vinegar, and seasoning. Toss the salad and garnish with the reserved basil leaves.

For summer chicken wraps, omit the potatoes and make the recipe up as above. Warm 4 soft tortillas as directed on the pack then spread with ¾ cup hummus. Toss the griddled chicken, cut into strips, and vegetables with 2 tablespoons olive oil, the balsamic vinegar as above, and reserved basil leaves. Divide between the tortillas then roll up tightly and serve cut in half while the chicken is still warm.

barbecued chicken with apple slaw

Serves **4**
Preparation time **25 minutes**
Cooking time **15 minutes**

6 tablespoons **tomato
ketchup**
2 tablespoons **Worcestershire
sauce**
2 tablespoons **red wine
vinegar**
2 tablespoons **light brown
sugar**
2 teaspoons **English mustard**
12 **chicken wings**

For the apple slaw
1 **dessert apple**, cored, diced
1 tablespoon **lemon juice**
1 **carrot**, coarsely grated
3 **scallions**, thinly sliced
2 cups finely shredded **white
cabbage**, core discarded
6 tablespoons **light
mayonnaise**
salt and **pepper**

Mix the ketchup, Worcestershire sauce, vinegar, sugar, and mustard together. Put the chicken on a foil-lined baking sheet or broiler rack, then brush with the ketchup mixture.

Cook the chicken wings under a preheated broiler or on a barbecue for about 15 minutes, turning once or twice until a deep brown and the chicken is cooked through. Test the chicken (see page 11).

Meanwhile, mix all the slaw ingredients together in a bowl, then spoon into a bowl. Put the chicken wings onto a plate and serve with plenty of paper napkins for sticky fingers.

For Chinese barbecued chicken wings, mix 4 tablespoons hoisin sauce with 4 tablespoons orange juice, 2 tablespoons Chinese rice wine or dry sherry, and 2 tablespoons tomato ketchup. Brush over the chicken and grill or broil as above.

chicken club sandwich

Serves **4**
Preparation time **15 minutes**
Cooking time **10 minutes**

4 small boneless, skinless
  chicken breasts, thinly
  sliced
8 slices **bacon**
1 tablespoon **sunflower oil**
12 slices **bread**
4 tablespoons **light
  mayonnaise**
4 oz **dolcelatte** or **bleu
  d'Auvergne cheese**, thinly
  sliced
4 **tomatoes**, thinly sliced
1 cup **watercress**

Fry the chicken and bacon in the oil for 6–8 minutes,
turning once or twice until golden and the chicken is
cooked through.

Toast the bread on both sides, then spread with the
mayonnaise. Divide the chicken and bacon between
four slices of toast, then top with the sliced cheese.
Cover the cheese with 4 more slices of toast, then
add the tomato slices and watercress. Complete the
sandwich stacks with the final slices of toast.

Press the sandwiches together, then cut each stack
into 4 small triangles. Secure with toothpicks, if
needed, and serve immediately.

For deli deluxe chicken sandwich, fry the chicken in
the oil as above, omitting the bacon. Split and toast
the cut sides of a ciabatta loaf, spread the lower half
with 4 teaspoons of black-olive tapenade, then top
with 2 tablespoons of mayonnaise. Add the chicken
to the tapenade toast, cover with 4 oz sliced brie
cheese, then 3 oz sundried tomatoes and 1 cup
arugula leaves. Top with the remaining toast, then
cut into 4 thick slices. Serve warm.

chicken with peanut sauce

Serves **4**
Preparation time **5 minutes**
Cooking time **16–20 minutes**

4 x 4 oz boneless, skinless
  chicken breasts
1 tablespoon **soy sauce**
2 tablespoons **crunchy** or
  smooth peanut butter
4 tablespoons **lemon juice**
4 tablespoons **water**
pepper

To garnish
cilantro leaves
peanuts, fried, chopped
  (optional)

Heat a griddle pan (or ordinary skillet). Place the chicken breasts in the pan and cook for 8–10 minutes on each side.

Meanwhile, place the soy sauce, peanut butter, lemon juice, water, and a little pepper in a small saucepan. Mix well and heat gently, adjusting the consistency of the sauce with a little more water if necessary, so that it is slightly runny but coats the back of a spoon.

When the chicken is cooked, serve with the peanut sauce drizzled over the top, garnished with cilantro and chopped fried peanuts, if desired. Serve with mixed vegetable noodles.

For egg fried rice, to serve as an alternative accompaniment, add 1¼ cups long-grain rice to a saucepan of boiling water. Simmer for 8 minutes, then add 1 cup frozen peas and cook for 2 minutes before draining. Heat 1 teaspoon sunflower oil in a skillet, add 2 beaten eggs and make a thin omelet. Roll the omelet up, shred, and mix with the cooked rice.

miso chicken broth

Serves **4**

Preparation time **10 minutes**

Cooking time **16–18 minutes**

1 tablespoon **sunflower oil**

2 boneless, skinless **chicken breasts**, diced

8 oz **cup mushrooms**, sliced

1 **carrot**, cut into thin matchsticks

¾ inch piece **ginger root**, grated

2 large pinches **dried red pepper flakes**

2 tablespoons **brown rice miso paste**

4 tablespoons **mirin** or **dry sherry**

2 tablespoons **light soy sauce**

5 cups **water**

2 **bok choy**, thinly sliced

4 **scallions**, thinly sliced

4 tablespoons chopped **cilantro**

Heat the oil in a saucepan, add the chicken, and fry for 4–5 minutes, stirring until golden. Add the mushrooms and carrot sticks, then the ginger, pepper flakes, miso, mirin or sherry, and soy sauce.

Pour on the water and bring to a boil, stirring. Simmer for 10 minutes.

Add the bok choy, scallions, and chopped cilantro and cook for 2–3 minutes until the bok choy has just wilted. Spoon into bowls and serve.

For hot & sour chicken soup, fry the chicken in oil as above, add 1½ cups sliced mushrooms and 1 carrot, cut into matchsticks. Flavor with 2 finely chopped garlic cloves, 3 teaspoons red Thai curry paste, 1 tablespoon Thai fish sauce, and 2 tablespoons light soy sauce. Add 5 cups chicken stock (see page 10), bring to a boil, and cook for 10 minutes. Add 4 oz sliced mini corn ears, 2 oz sliced snow peas, and scallions and cilantro as above. Cook for 2–3 minutes. Ladle into bowls and serve with lime wedges.

chicken tacos & hot green salsa

Serves **4**
Preparation time **10 minutes**
Cooking time **16–20 minutes**

1 tablespoon **sunflower oil**
4 x 6 oz boneless, skinless
chicken breasts

For the hot green salsa
1 **avocado**, chopped
1 **red onion**, finely chopped
1–2 **hot green** or **red chilies**,
very finely chopped
1 **garlic clove**, very finely
chopped
1 bunch **cilantro**, roughly
chopped
4 tablespoons **lime juice**
4 tablespoons **olive oil**
salt and **pepper**

To serve
16 **taco shells**
⅔ cup **sour cream**

Heat a griddle pan (or ordinary skillet). Brush the chicken breasts with sunflower oil, place them in the pan and cook for 8–10 minutes on each side. Remove from the pan and slice into strips.

To make the salsa, place the avocado in a bowl and add the onion, chilies, garlic, and cilantro. Mix together, adding the lime juice, olive oil, and seasoning.

Pile some of the salsa in each of the taco shells and top with a few strips of chicken. Serve the remaining salsa separately, with a bowl of sour cream to spoon on top of the tacos just before eating.

For sweet potato jackets with chicken & tomato salsa, scrub and prick 4 medium-size sweet potatoes then bake at 400°F, for 50–60 minutes. Fry the chicken as above then dice. Make the salsa using 2 diced tomatoes in place of the avocado. Split the potatoes, top with spoonfuls of sour cream, chicken, and salsa.

seared chicken & vegetable wraps

Serves **4**
Preparation time **5 minutes**
Cooking time **12–15 minutes**

4 boneless, skinless **chicken breasts**, cut into long thin slices
4 **zucchini**, cut into long thin slices
1 **red bell pepper**, cored, seeded, quartered
1 **yellow bell pepper**, cored, seeded, quartered
4 tablespoons **olive oil**
2 **garlic cloves**, finely chopped
4 teaspoons **sundried tomato paste**
4 large **soft flour tortillas**
¾ cup **cream cheese with garlic and herbs**
salt and **pepper**

Arrange the chicken breasts, zucchini, and peppers in a single layer on a foil-lined broiler rack or baking sheet.

Mix the oil, garlic, tomato paste, and seasoning together and spoon over the chicken and vegetables. Broil for 12–15 minutes, turning once, until browned and the chicken is cooked through.

Warm the tortillas according to the instructions on the package, then spread with the cream cheese. Cut the peppers into strips, peeling if desired. Divide the chicken and vegetables between the tortillas, then roll up tightly and cut in half. Serve warm.

For Chinese chicken wraps, broil the chicken drizzled with a mixture made from 2 tablespoons sunflower oil, 2 finely chopped garlic gloves, 2 teaspoons ordinary tomato paste and ¼ teaspoon ground Chinese 5-spice powder. Spread 6 tablespoons hoisin sauce over 4 warmed tortillas, then top with the chicken, 1 bunch of scallions, cut into long thin strips, and ½ cucumber, seeded and cut into long thin sticks. Roll up and halve as above.

chicken picnic terrine

Serves **8**
Preparation time **40 minutes**,
  plus chilling
Cooking time **1 hour**
  35 minutes

10 oz **bacon**
1 tablespoon **olive oil**
1 **onion**, finely chopped
8 **Toulouse sausages**, about
  1 lb 2 oz, skins removed
4 oz **chicken livers**, defrosted
  if frozen, diced
4 boneless, skinless **chicken**
  thighs, cut into small dice
1 **Granny Smith dessert**
  apple, cored, coarsely
  grated
¼ teaspoon **grated nutmeg**
½ cup whole **pistachio nuts**
1 cup **fresh bread crumbs**
4 tablespoons **dry sherry**
  or **brandy**
salt and **pepper**

Use a strip of nonstick parchment paper to line the base and short sides of a 2 lb loaf pan. Stretch each bacon slice so it is half as long again, then butt close together to line the pan. Cut slices in half to line the ends of the pan, and set aside a few slices.

Heat the oil in a skillet, add the onion and fry for 5 minutes until softened.

Mix the sausagemeat, chicken livers, chicken thighs, apple, nutmeg, nuts, bread crumbs, and sherry or brandy in a large bowl, then stir in the onions and seasoning. Spoon the mixture into the bacon-lined pan, pressing it down well.

Fold the ends of the bacon over the top, then cover the gaps with the reserved slices. Cover with foil, stand the pan in a roasting pan and pour in hot water to come halfway up the sides. Cook in a preheated oven, 350°F, for 1½ hours or until cooked when tested (see page 11).

Tip the water out of the roasting pan. Cool the terrine then cover top of the loaf pan with weights and chill overnight. Loosen the edges of the terrine, turn it out of the pan and peel away the lining paper. Cut into thick slices and serve with radishes.

For pickled walnut, apricot, & chicken terrine, use herb sausages and mix as above, replacing the pistachios with 2 drained and roughly chopped pickled walnuts and ⅓ cup ready-to-eat dried apricots, chopped. Finish as above.

chicken liver & pomegranate salad

Serves **4**
Preparation time **10 minutes**
Cooking time **8–9 minutes**

2½ cups **mixed salad leaves with baby red Swiss chard**
2 small **crisphead lettuces**, leaves separated
2 x 8 oz packs frozen **chicken livers**, just defrosted
¼ cup **butter**
2 tablespoons **olive oil**
1 **red onion**, sliced
2 **garlic cloves**, finely chopped
4 tablespoons **vodka** or **brandy**
½ **pomegranate**
salt and **pepper**

Rinse the salad leaves in a colander, then drain well and divide between 4 serving plates, tearing any large lettuce leaves into bite-size pieces.

Rinse the chicken livers in the colander, drain well, then roughly chop, discarding any white cores.

Heat the butter and oil in a large skillet, add the onion and fry for 5 minutes until softened. Add the chicken livers and garlic and fry for 3–4 minutes until browned but still slightly pink in the center.

Add the alcohol; as soon as it begins to bubble, light it with a long match, then stand back. As soon as the flames subside, season well, then spoon over the salad. Flex the pomegranate so that the seeds pop out, then sprinkle these over the salad and serve.

For chicken liver toasts, finely chop the onions and chicken livers, then fry as above. When cooked, spoon onto 12 slices of toasted French bread, and sprinkle with chopped parsley and a few chopped midget gherkins. Serve hot as an appetizer with drinks.

griddled chicken fajitas

Serves **4**

Preparation time **20 minutes**, plus marinating

Cooking time **16–20 minutes**

4 x 4 oz boneless, skinless **chicken breasts**

4 large **soft flour tortillas**

⅔ cup **sour cream**

4 **tomatoes**, skinned and sliced

1 **avocado**, sliced

4 **scallions**, sliced

½ **red onion**, finely chopped

tortilla chips, to serve (optional)

salt and **pepper**

For the marinade

2 tablespoons **soy sauce**

1¼ inch piece **ginger root**, finely chopped

2 **garlic cloves**, finely chopped

2 tablespoons **olive oil**

1 bunch **cilantro**, chopped

1 **chili**, chopped

2 tablespoons **lime juice**

Combine all the ingredients for the marinade in a shallow dish. Add the chicken breasts and allow to marinate at room temperature for 2 hours, or in the refrigerator for 24 hours.

Heat a griddle pan (or ordinary skillet). Place the marinated chicken breasts in the pan to cook for 8–10 minutes on each side. When cooked, remove the chicken from the pan and slice it into long strips.

Place the tortillas under a preheated broiler and cook for 30 seconds on each side. Spread over one side of each tortilla a spoonful of sour cream, a little tomato, avocado, and a sprinkling of scallions and red onion.

Add the pieces of griddled chicken and season. Roll up each tortilla tightly and cut in half across each one. Serve with tortilla chips, if desired.

For guacamole, to accompany the fajitas, halve and pit 2 ripe avocados. Scoop out the flesh then mash with a fork. Mix with the juice of 1 lime, 3 tablespoons chopped cilantro, 1 skinned and finely diced tomato, and, if desired, 1 finely chopped jalapeno chili. Spoon onto the tortillas instead of sour cream.

chicken & vegetable skewers

Serves **4**

Preparation time **10 minutes**

Cooking time **15 minutes**

4 **chicken thighs**, skinned and boned

2 tablespoons **honey**

2 tablespoons **mild wholegrain mustard**

1 **zucchini**, cut into 8 large pieces

1 **carrot**, cut into 8 large pieces

Cut the chicken thighs into bite-size pieces and toss in the honey and mustard. Arrange the chicken pieces on a baking sheet and bake in a preheated oven, 350°F, for 15 minutes until cooked through and lightly golden. Set aside and allow to cool.

Take 8 bamboo skewers and thread with the cooked chicken pieces and the raw vegetables.

Serve with the honey and mustard mixture for dipping. The skewers can also be refrigerated for adding to the following day's lunchbox.

For sticky chicken with honey & garlic, mix together 2 tablespoons tomato ketchup, 2 teaspoons honey, 2 finely chopped garlic cloves and 1 tablespoon of sunflower oil. Dip the chicken into the ketchup mixture then cook as above. Thread onto skewers with 1 red bell pepper, seeded, cored, and cut into chunks and 8 cherry tomatoes.

chicken, tarragon, & orange salad

Serves **4**
Preparation time **20 minutes**
Cooking time **45 minutes–
   1 hour**

3 lb **whole chicken**
1 medium **onion**, thinly sliced
grated zest and juice of
   1 **orange**
1 tablespoon chopped fresh
   tarragon (or 1 teaspoon
   dried)
1 **bay leaf**
1 tablespoon **olive oil**
½–1 tablespoon **white wine
   vinegar**
salt and **pepper**

To garnish
1 small **orange**, thinly sliced
small bunch **mustard and
   cress**
tarragon sprigs (optional)

Put the chicken, onion, orange zest and juice, tarragon, and bay leaf in a large saucepan. Pour enough water over the top of the chicken to cover it and sprinkle with salt and pepper to taste. Cover, bring to a boil, and simmer for 1–1¼ hours, until the chicken is cooked.

Lift the chicken out of the saucepan and allow to cool. Discard the bay leaf and onion. Measure the stock, then boil until it reduces to ⅔ cup. Set aside to cool, then chill in the refrigerator.

When the chicken is cold, take the meat off the bones, discarding the skin. Cut the meat into bite-size pieces and place in a bowl.

When the stock has chilled, remove the layer of fat from the top, then reheat gently to thin it. Stir in the oil, add the vinegar, and season to taste. Pour this dressing over the chicken and toss well.

Serve immediately, garnished with orange slices, mustard, cress, and tarragon sprigs, if desired, or cover and chill until required. The salad may also be served on a bed of shredded iceberg lettuce.

For chicken, tarragon, & orange tagliatelle, add ⅔ cup heavy cream to the cooled and reduced stock. Stir in the diced chicken then reheat. Add ¾ cup torn watercress and cook for 1 minute until the leaves just wilt. Toss with just-cooked tagliatelle.

chicken picnic loaf

Serves **12**
Preparation time **20 minutes**,
  plus marinating and chilling
Cooking time **20 minutes**

4 boneless, skinless **chicken
  breasts**, skinned
4 boneless **chicken thigh
  pieces**, skinned
1 tablespoon **lemon juice**
½ teaspoon **ground turmeric**
2 tablespoons **olive oil**
5 tablespoons **water**
3 tablespoons chopped fresh
  mixed herbs
½ cup **pistachio nuts**, toasted
  and roughly chopped
1 large round Eastern-style
  sesame loaf
8 oz **chicken liver pâté**
salt and **pepper**

Rub the chicken pieces all over with the lemon juice,
turmeric, and half the oil, and season. Allow to marinate
for 1 hour.

Heat the remaining oil in a skillet and fry the chicken
for 5 minutes until golden on both sides. Add the
measured water, bring to a boil, then cover and simmer
gently for 15 minutes. Allow to cool in the pan.

Remove the chicken and cut it into strips, reserving
the pan juices. Place the chicken in a bowl and stir in
the herbs, nuts, and reserved juices.

Cut the top from the sesame loaf and scoop out the
middle, leaving a 1 inch thick shell. (You could make
bread crumbs from the filling and freeze for later use
if you desire.)

Spoon half the chicken into the hollow bread and
carefully spread the pâté over the top. Add the
remaining chicken and replace the bread lid. Wrap
the loaf tightly in plastic wrap, weigh down with a
heavy object, and allow to chill overnight. Cut into
wedges to serve.

For chicken & pistachio couscous, marinade then
fry the chicken as above. Mix with the herbs, nuts,
and reserved juices. Mix 2 teaspoons harissa paste
with 2 cups boiling water. Add 1 cup couscous
and allow to soak for 5 minutes. Stir in the juice
of ½ lemon, 2 chopped tomatoes, and then the
chicken and nut mix, before serving.

easy
suppers

chicken caldo verde

Serves **4**
Preparation time **20 minutes**
Cooking time **44–45 minutes**

2 tablespoons **olive oil**
1 **onion**, roughly chopped
4 oz piece **chorizo**, skinned,
  diced or sliced depending
  on diameter
8 **chicken thighs**, boned,
  skinned, cubed
1 lb **baking potatoes**,
  scrubbed, cubed
1 **garlic clove**, finely chopped
1 teaspoon **smoked paprika**
3 cups **chicken stock**
  (see page 10)
13 oz can **cranberry beans**,
  drained
1½ cups **curly kale leaves**
crusty bread, to serve
salt and **pepper**

Heat the oil in a large saucepan, add the onion and chorizo and fry for 5 minutes, stirring occasionally until the onion has softened. Add the chicken and fry for 5 more minutes until lightly browned.

Mix in the potatoes, garlic, and paprika and cook for 1 minute, then add the stock, beans, and a little salt and pepper. Bring to a boil, then cover and simmer for 30 minutes until the potatoes are tender.

Tear the kale into bite-size pieces, add to the pan, and push beneath the surface of the stock. Cook for 3–4 minutes until just wilted. Ladle into shallow bowls and serve with warm crusty bread.

For chicken caldo verde with pistou, replace the smoked paprika with 2 teaspoons pesto sauce, use navy beans instead of cranberry beans, and use ¾ cup sliced green beans instead of the kale.

chicken with sage & lemon

Serves **4**

Preparation time **15 minutes**,
  plus marinating

Cooking time **20 minutes**

4 boneless, skinless **chicken
  breasts**, about 5 oz each

5 tablespoons **olive oil**

3 tablespoons **lemon juice**

28 small **sage leaves**

3 tablespoons **unsalted
  butter**

cooked puy lentils, to serve
  (optional)

salt and **pepper**

Place the chicken breasts in a single layer in a nonmetallic dish. Pour over 3 tablespoons of the oil, and the lemon juice. Sprinkle with the sage leaves, turn the chicken so that the breasts are evenly coated, then cover and allow to marinate for about 30 minutes.

Lift the chicken breasts from the marinade and reserve the sage leaves separately. Pat the breasts dry. Strain the marinade into a small bowl.

Heat the butter and the remaining oil in a skillet, add the chicken, and cook for about 10 minutes over a moderate heat until browned. Turn the chicken breasts over, season with salt and pepper, and tuck the sage leaves around them. Cook for an additional 10 minutes until the underside is brown and the chicken is cooked through. Transfer the chicken to a warmed serving plate, cover, and keep warm.

Tilt the pan and pour off the fat. Place the pan back on the heat and stir in the reserved marinade, scraping up any brown bits from the bottom of the pan. Boil until reduced to a brown glaze. Serve the chicken in slices, on a bed of puy lentils, if desired. Pour the remaining marinade over the chicken and garnish with the sage leaves.

For garlic & lemon mash, as an alternative to the lentil accompaniment, boil 1½ lb potatoes until tender. Drain and mash with ¼ cup butter, the grated zest and juice of ½ lemon, and 3 finely chopped garlic cloves.

mojo chicken

Serves **4**
Preparation time **25 minutes**, plus marinating
Cooking time **10–12 minutes**

grated zest and juice of 1 small **orange**
grated zest and juice of 1 **lime**
1 tablespoon **sunflower oil**
1 large **mild red chili**, seeded, finely chopped
2 **garlic cloves**, finely chopped
2 teaspoons **light brown sugar**
1 teaspoon **cumin seeds**, roughly crushed
4 boneless, skinless **chicken breasts**, cubed
lemon wedges, to garnish

For the guacamole
2 ripe **avocados**
grated zest and juice of 1 **lime**
small bunch **cilantro**, roughly snipped
salt and **pepper**

Mix the fruit zests and juice, oil, chili, garlic, sugar, cumin, and a little seasoning together in a shallow china or glass dish. Add the chicken and toss together well. Cover with plastic wrap, marinate in the refrigerator for 2 hours (or longer if you have time).

When ready to serve, thread the chicken onto 8 wooden or thin metal skewers. Cook under a hot broiler, turning several times for 10–12 minutes until browned and cooked through.

Meanwhile, to make the guacamole, halve and pit the avocados and scoop the flesh out of the skin with a spoon. Roughly mash on a plate or in a food processor with the lime zest and juice. Season and stir in half the cilantro.

Serve the skewers on plates garnished with the remaining cilantro, lemon wedges, spoonfuls of guacamole, and small bowls of salad and roasted sweet potatoes.

For citrus chicken wraps, cut the chicken into strips and marinate as above. Lift out of the marinade and fry in 1 tablespoon sunflower oil for 6–8 minutes until golden. Divide between 4 large soft flour tortillas, adding ½ crisp lettuce, finely shredded, 1 thinly sliced red onion, and spoonfuls of the guacamole. Roll up tightly, then cut each one in half. Serve warm.

chicken cacciatore

Serves **4**
Preparation time **10 minutes**
Cooking time **20 minutes**

4 boneless, skinless **chicken
  breasts**, each about 4 oz
1 lb **cherry** or **mini plum
  tomatoes**, halved
1 **red onion**, cut into wedges
2 **garlic cloves**, finely chopped
2–3 stems **rosemary**, torn
  into pieces
6 tablespoons **red wine**
2 tablespoons **balsamic
  vinegar**
8 oz **dried linguine** or
  fettuccine
2 tablespoons grated
  **fat-reduced mature
  cheddar cheese** (optional)
pepper

Arrange the chicken in a large roasting pan or
ovenproof dish so that it lies in a single layer. Add
the tomatoes and onion, then sprinkle over the garlic
and rosemary. Drizzle with the wine and vinegar and
add a little pepper.

Bake in a preheated oven, 425°F, for 20 minutes or
until the onions and chicken are browned and the
juices run clear when the chicken is pierced with
a skewer.

Halfway through cooking, bring a large saucepan
of water to a boil, add the pasta, and cook for
8–10 minutes until just tender.

Drain the pasta and return to the empty pan. Slice
the chicken breasts and add to the pasta with the
onions, tomatoes, and pan juices. Toss together and
spoon into bowls. Sprinkle with a little rosemary and
top with grated cheese, if desired.

For roast chicken & white bean salad, roast the
chicken with the other ingredients as above, but
rather than serving with pasta, mix with a 13½ oz
drained can of navy or cannellini beans. Allow to
cool then stir and toss with 1 cup mixed spinach,
arugula, and watercress salad.

chicken pimenton with puy lentils

Serves **4**
Preparation time **20 minutes**
Cooking time **20 minutes**

1 cup **puy lentils**
3 tablespoons **olive oil**
6 **chicken thighs**, skinned,
  boned, cut into cubes
1 **red onion**, halved, sliced
1 tablespoon chopped
  rosemary leaves
¼ teaspoon **smoked paprika
  (pimenton)**
8 oz **cherry tomatoes**, halved
2 tablespoons **balsamic
  vinegar**, plus a little extra
2½ cups **baby spinach
  leaves**, rinsed, drained
salt and **pepper**

Add the lentils to a saucepan of boiling water and simmer for 15–20 minutes until just tender. Meanwhile, heat 1 tablespoon of the oil in a large skillet, add the chicken and onion and fry for 10 minutes, stirring until the chicken is browned.

Stir in the rosemary and paprika and cook for 1 minute, then mix in the tomatoes and seasoning and cook for 3–4 minutes, stirring until the tomatoes are just beginning to soften.

Drain the lentils into a sieve, add the remaining oil, vinegar, and seasoning to the base of the dry pan and mix together. Return the lentils to the pan and mix in the spinach. Cook for 1 minute, stirring until the spinach is just beginning to wilt.

Spoon the lentil and spinach mixture onto serving plates and top with the chicken mix. Drizzle with a little extra balsamic vinegar, if desired. Serve immediately.

For creamy chicken rigatoni, omit the lentils. Cook the chicken and onion as above, adding paprika and rosemary. Add the spinach and when just wilted stir in ⅔ cup heavy cream. Cook 12 oz rigatoni pasta in boiling water until tender, then drain and stir into the cream mixture, heat through, and serve in shallow bowls.

citrus chicken & fruited bulghur

Serves **4**
Preparation time **25 minutes**
Cooking time **12–17 minutes**

3½ cups **chicken stock**
   (see page 10)
¼ teaspoon **ground cinnamon**
¼ teaspoon **ground nutmeg**
   or **allspice**
1¼ cups **bulghur wheat**
4 boneless, skinless **chicken
   breasts**, about 5 oz each
grated zest of ½ **lemon**
grated zest of ½ **orange**
⅔ cup ready-to-eat **dried
   apricots**
½ cup pitted **dates**, chopped
½ cup **golden raisins**
juice of 1 **orange**
small bunch **cilantro** or **basil**,
   torn, to garnish
salt and **pepper**

Pour the stock into the base of a steamer and add the ground spices and bulghur wheat.

Rinse the chicken breasts with cold water, drain them, then place in the steamer top and sprinkle with the lemon and orange zest and a little salt and pepper.

Bring the stock to a boil, put the steamer top in place, cover with a lid, and cook for about 10 minutes until the chicken is thoroughly cooked and the bulghur is tender. Remove the steamer top and cook the bulghur for a few extra minutes if needed.

Stir the dried fruits and orange juice into the bulghur, then spoon the bulghur and any stock onto 4 plates. Slice the chicken pieces, arrange over the bulghur and garnish with torn herb leaves. Serve with a watercress and arugula salad.

For citrus chicken salad, steam the chicken with the fruit zests and seasoning over a pan of simmering water. Cool then dice. Coarsely grate 2 carrots, peel and segment 2 oranges, slice 4 oz fresh pitted dates. Arrange on a serving plate with the leaves torn from 1 small crisphead lettuce. Mix the juice of ½ lemon with 1 teaspoon superfine sugar, 1 tablespoon orange flower water, and a little salt. Drizzle this over the salad and garnish with torn cilantro.

chicken arrabiata

Serves **4**
Preparation time **20 minutes**
Cooking time **36 minutes**

1 tablespoon **olive oil**
1 **onion**, roughly chopped
8 **chicken thighs**, boned,
  skinned, cut into cubes
2 **garlic cloves**, finely
  chopped
1 teaspoon **smoked paprika**
¼–½ teaspoon **dried red
  pepper flakes**, to taste
13 oz can **chopped tomatoes**
1 cup **chicken stock**
  (see page 10)
12 oz **macaroni**
large handful **arugula leaves**,
  to garnish
Parmesan cheese, grated or
  shaved, to serve (optional)
salt and **pepper**

Heat the oil in a large saucepan, add the onion and fry for 5 minutes, stirring occasionally until softened. Add the chicken and fry for 5 more minutes until lightly browned.

Mix in the garlic, paprika, and pepper flakes and cook for 1 minute, then stir in the tomatoes, stock, and a little salt and pepper. Bring to a boil, then cover and simmer for 25 minutes until the chicken is tender.

Meanwhile, half-fill a second pan with water, bring to a boil, then add the macaroni. Simmer for 10–12 minutes until just tender, then drain.

Stir the macaroni into the sauce and reheat if needed. Spoon into shallow bowls and garnish with the arugula leaves. Serve with grated Parmesan, if desired.

For chicken puttanesca, omit the pepper flakes and add 1 red bell pepper, cored, seeded, and diced, 2 teaspoons drained capers and ½ cup marinated green and black olives. Toss with 12 oz just-cooked spaghetti and sprinkle with grated Parmesan.

thai barbecued chicken

Serves **4–6**

Preparation time **20–25 minutes**, plus chilling time

Cooking time **30–40 minutes or 10–15 minutes**, depending on type of chicken

3 lb **whole chicken**, spatchcocked (see page 15), or part-boned **chicken breasts**

2 inch piece **galangal**, peeled, finely chopped

4 **garlic cloves**, crushed

1 large **red chili**, finely chopped

4 **shallots**, finely chopped

2 tablespoons finely chopped **cilantro leaves**

⅔ cup **thick coconut milk**

chive flowers, to garnish

lime wedges, to serve

salt and **pepper**

Rub the chicken all over with salt and pepper and place in a shallow container.

Put the galangal, garlic, red chili, shallots, and cilantro in a food processor and blend to a paste, or use a mortar and pestle. Add the coconut milk and mix until well blended. Pour over the chicken, cover, and allow to marinate overnight in the refrigerator.

Remove the chicken from the marinade, place it on a hot barbecue and cook for 30–40 minutes for spatchcocked chicken and 10–15 minutes for chicken breasts, turning and basting regularly with the remaining marinade. The whole chicken is cooked when a skewer inserted in one of the legs reveals clear juices.

Allow the chicken to stand for 5 minutes, then chop it into small pieces with a cleaver. Garnish with chive flowers and eat with fingers. Serve with lime wedges, as well as a dipping sauce and sticky rice, if desired.

For sweet chili sauce to serve as an accompaniment, wearing a pair of plastic gloves remove the seeds from 15 medium red chilies and finely chop the flesh. Place the chilies in a saucepan with 1 cup granulated sugar, ⅔ cup rice wine vinegar, and ⅔ cup water. Heat gently to dissolve the sugar, then increase the heat and simmer briskly for 20–25 minutes or until the liquid has reduced to a syrup. Pour the sauce into a sterilized glass jar or bottle and keep in the refrigerator until required.

catalan chicken

Serves **4**
Preparation time **15 minutes**
Cooking time **25 minutes**

2 tablespoons **olive oil**
½ cup **slivered almonds**
2 **onions**, roughly chopped
8 **chicken thighs**, boned,
  skinned, cubed
2 **garlic cloves**, finely
  chopped
⅔ cup **raisins**
¾ cup **dry sherry**
1 cup **chicken stock**
  (see page 10)
small bunch **flat-leaf parsley**,
  roughly chopped
salt and **pepper**

Heat a little of the oil in a large skillet, add the almonds and fry, stirring for a few minutes until golden. Scoop out of the pan and set aside.

Add the remaining oil to the pan, then add the onions, chicken, and garlic and fry over a medium heat for 10 minutes, stirring until deep golden. Mix in the raisins, sherry, stock, and a little salt and pepper.

Simmer for 10 minutes until the sauce has reduced slightly and the chicken is cooked through. Sprinkle with the parsley and serve with rice and salad.

For Normandy chicken, omit the raisins and add 1 cored and diced Granny Smith dessert apple and 2 teaspoons Dijon mustard, replacing the sherry with ¾ cup dry hard cider. Serve topped with spoonfuls of sour cream.

chicken skewers with couscous

Serves **4**

Preparation time **25 minutes**,
  plus chilling time

Cooking time **20–25 minutes**

1 lb boneless, skinless
  chicken breasts

2 tablespoons **olive oil**

2 **garlic cloves**, crushed

½ teaspoon each **ground
  cumin, turmeric, paprika**

2 teaspoons **lemon juice**

For the couscous

4 tablespoons **olive oil**

1 small **onion**, finely chopped

1 **garlic clove**, crushed

1 teaspoon each **ground
  cumin, cinnamon, pepper,
  ginger**

⅓ cup **dried dates**

⅓ cup **dried apricots**

⅓ cup **blanched almonds**,
  toasted

2½ cups **vegetable stock**,
  boiling

1 cup **couscous**

1 tablespoon **lemon juice**

2 tablespoons chopped
  cilantro leaves

salt and **pepper**

Cut the chicken into long thin strips, place them in a shallow dish, and add the olive oil, garlic, spices, and lemon juice. Stir well, then cover and allow to marinate for 2 hours. Thread the chicken strips onto 8 small, presoaked wooden skewers.

Prepare the couscous by heating half the oil in a saucepan and frying the onion, garlic, and spices for 5 minutes. Chop and stir in the dried fruits and almonds and remove from the heat.

Meanwhile, put the couscous in a heatproof bowl, add the boiling stock and cover with a dish towel and steam for 8–10 minutes, until the grains are fluffed up and the liquid absorbed. Stir in the remaining oil and the fruit and nut mixture, add the lemon juice and cilantro and season to taste.

While the couscous is steaming, griddle or broil the chicken skewers for 4–5 minutes on each side, until charred and cooked through. Serve with the couscous, garnished with pomegranate seeds, lemon wedges, and cilantro sprigs, if desired.

For roasted chicken with herb couscous, mix the oil, garlic, spices, and lemon juice and drizzle over 8 skinned and slashed chicken thighs. Roast at 375°F, for 35–45 minutes. Steam the couscous as above in stock. Stir in the remaining oil and lemon juice. Add 4 finely chopped scallions, 3 tablespoons chopped mint, 3 tablespoons chopped parsley, and 2 chopped tomatoes. Spoon onto plates, top with the chicken, and serve with lemon wedges.

speedy spiced chicken tagine

Serves **4**

Preparation time **20 minutes**

Cooking time **55 minutes**

1 tablespoon **olive oil**

8 **chicken thighs**, skinned

1 **onion**, sliced

2 **garlic cloves**, finely
chopped

1 lb **plum tomatoes**, skinned
(optional), cut into chunks

1 teaspoon **turmeric**

1 **cinnamon stick**, halved

1 inch piece **ginger root**,
grated

2 teaspoons **honey**

½ cup ready-to-eat **dried
apricots**, quartered

1 cup **couscous**

1¾ cups **boiling water**

grated zest and juice of
1 **lemon**

small bunch **cilantro**, roughly
chopped

salt and **pepper**

Heat the oil in a large skillet, add the chicken and fry until browned on both sides. Lift out and transfer to a tagine or casserole dish. Add the onion to the pan and fry until golden.

Stir in the garlic, tomatoes, spices, and honey. Add the apricots and a little salt and pepper and heat through. Spoon over the chicken, cover the dish, and bake in a preheated oven, 350°F, for 45 minutes or until the chicken is cooked through.

When the chicken is almost ready, soak the couscous in boiling water for 5 minutes. Stir in the lemon zest and juice, cilantro, and seasoning. Spoon onto plates and top with the chicken and tomatoes, discarding the cinnamon stick just before eating.

For chicken & vegetable stew, use just 4 chicken thigh joints and add 1 diced carrot, 1 cored, seeded, and diced red bell pepper and 1 cup frozen fava beans. Replace the cinnamon with 2 teaspoons harissa paste and add ⅔ cup chicken stock (see page 10). Cook as above, adding 4 oz thickly sliced okra or green beans for the last 15 minutes of cooking. Sprinkle with chopped cilantro or mint and serve with rice.

chicken with spinach & ricotta

Serves **4**
Preparation time **5 minutes**
Cooking time **25 minutes**

4 boneless, skinless **chicken
  breasts**, 4 oz each
½ cup **ricotta cheese**
⅓ cup cooked **spinach**,
  squeezed dry
¼ teaspoon grated **nutmeg**
8 slices **prosciutto**
2 tablespoons **olive oil**, plus
  extra for drizzling
salt and **pepper**

To serve
lemon wedges
arugula leaves

Make a long horizontal slit through the thickest part of
each chicken breast without cutting right through.

Crumble the ricotta into a bowl. Chop the spinach and
mix into the ricotta with the nutmeg. Season with salt
and pepper.

Divide the stuffing between the slits in the chicken
breasts and wrap each one in 2 pieces of prosciutto,
winding it around the chicken to cover the meat totally.

Heat the oil in a shallow ovenproof pan, add the
chicken breasts and sauté for 4 minutes on each
side or until the ham starts to brown. Transfer to a
preheated oven, 400°F, and cook for 15 minutes.
Serve with lemon wedges and arugula leaves drizzled
with olive oil.

For chicken with mozzarella & sundried tomatoes,
instead of the ricotta, spinach, and nutmeg, stuff
each chicken breast with a thick slice of mozzarella
and a sundried tomato piece, drained of its olive oil.
Season well with black pepper and continue as in
the main recipe.

chicken stew & dumplings

Serves **4**
Preparation time **30 minutes**
Cooking time **1 hour**
  15 minutes

8 boneless, skinless **chicken thighs**
1 tablespoon **sunflower oil**
1 **onion**, roughly chopped
2 **parsnips**, cut into chunks
2 **carrots**, cut into chunks
6 oz **rutabaga**, cut into chunks
¼ cup **pearl barley**
1½ cups **pale ale**
1¼ cups **chicken stock**
  (see page 10)
2 teaspoons prepared **English mustard**
salt and **pepper**

For the dumplings
1½ cups **self-rising flour**
¾ cup **light shredded suet**
4 tablespoons chopped **chives**
7–8 tablespoons **cold water**
salt and **pepper**

Cut each chicken thigh in half. Heat the oil in a flameproof casserole, add the chicken and onion and fry over a high heat until golden. Stir in the remaining vegetables and cook for 2 minutes, then mix in the barley, ale, stock, and mustard. Season and bring to a boil. Cover and transfer to a preheated oven, 350°F, for 1 hour.

When the chicken has finished cooking, make the dumplings by mixing the flour, suet, chives, and some seasoning in a bowl. Stir in enough water to mix to a soft, slightly sticky dough, then shape dessertspoons of the mixture into balls.

Stir the chicken stew and transfer to the stovetop. When the stock is boiling, add the dumplings, cover, and simmer for about 15 minutes or until the dumplings are light and fluffy. Spoon into shallow bowls to serve.

For chicken hotpot, omit the dumplings and cover the surface of the stew with 1¼ lb thinly sliced potatoes before it goes into the oven. Cover and cook for 1 hour, remove the lid, dot with 2 tablespoons butter, season, and cook for 30 minutes more until the potatoes are lightly browned.

lemon-infused chicken & spaghetti

Serves **4**

Preparation time **15 minutes**

Cooking time **16–20 minutes**

4 **lemons**

4 x 4 oz boneless, skinless **chicken breasts**

1 bunch **oregano**, chopped

10 oz **spaghetti**

1 bunch **parsley**, chopped

2 tablespoons **olive oil**

salt and **pepper**

Thinly slice 3 of the lemons, setting aside 8 large slices. Grate the zest and squeeze the juice from the fourth lemon, and set aside.

Using a sharp knife, make a pouch in the middle of each chicken breast. Fill each chicken pocket with the smaller slices of lemon, some chopped oregano leaves, and salt and pepper.

Heat a griddle pan (or ordinary skillet). Sandwich each chicken breast between 2 of the reserved large lemon slices and a sprig of oregano. Place the chicken in the pan and cook for 8–10 minutes on each side—try to keep the lemon intact with the chicken so that all the citrus flavor infuses into the chicken.

Meanwhile, bring a large saucepan of lightly salted water to a boil. When boiling, plunge the spaghetti into the water and cook for 12 minutes, or according to the instructions on the package. Drain well, then toss with the lemon zest and juice, the parsley, the olive oil, and seasoning to taste. Serve with the lemon chicken.

For lemon-infused chicken with arugula & lentil salad, omit the spaghetti and instead add ¾ cup puy lentils to a saucepan of boiling water. Simmer for 15–20 minutes or until tender. Cook the chicken with lemon slices and oregano as above. Add the remaining lemon juice, olive oil, and seasoning to the cooked lentils then add 1 cup arugula leaves instead of the parsley. Serve with the chicken.

sticky mustard chicken & potatoes

Serves **4**

Preparation time **20 minutes**, plus standing

Cooking time **30 minutes**

2 tablespoons **sherry vinegar**
1 tablespoon **sunflower oil**
1 tablespoon **honey**
2 teaspoons **wholegrain mustard**
¼ teaspoon **turmeric**
4 boneless, skinless **chicken breasts**, each about 5 oz
1lb 6 oz **new potatoes**
5 tablespoons **sour cream**
1¼ cups **mixed spinach, arugula, and watercress salad**, roughly chopped
salt and **pepper**

Mix the vinegar, oil, honey, mustard, and turmeric in a shallow ovenproof dish with a little seasoning. Add the chicken and turn until completely coated. Allow to stand for 10 minutes.

Turn the chicken once more, then roast, still in the same dish, in a preheated oven, 400°F, for 30 minutes until browned, spooning the glaze over halfway through cooking, and covering with foil if needed.

Meanwhile, cut any large potatoes in half and add to a saucepan of boiling water, then simmer for 15 minutes until tender. Drain and roughly crush with a fork, then mix with the sour cream, salad, and seasoning, then warm through.

Test the chicken (see page 11). When it is cooked through, spoon the potatoes onto plates, then top with the chicken, spooning over any remaining glaze.

For sticky marmalade chicken, mix 2 tablespoons chunky marmalade with a 1 inch piece peeled and grated ginger root, 2 finely chopped garlic cloves, 1 teaspoon Dijon mustard, the juice of ½ orange, and 1 tablespoon sunflower oil. Coat the chicken and bake as above. Serve with crushed new potatoes mixed with sour cream and ⅔ cup just-cooked frozen peas.

szechuan chicken

Serves **4**

Preparation time **5 minutes**,
  plus marinating

Cooking time **16–20 minutes**

3 tablespoons **soy sauce**

2 tablespoons **dry sherry**

1 teaspoon **rice vinegar**

1¼ inch piece **ginger root**,
  peeled and finely chopped

1 **garlic clove**, crushed

1 tablespoon **Chinese chili
  paste**

½ teaspoon **Szechuan
  peppercorns**, ground

1 tablespoon **dark sesame oil**

4 x 4 oz boneless, skinless
  chicken breasts

cilantro leaves, chopped,
  to garnish

Mix together all the ingredients except the chicken in a shallow dish to make the marinade. Add the chicken breasts, coat well with the marinade and allow to marinate at room temperature for 2 hours.

Heat a griddle pan (or ordinary skillet). Cook the chicken for 8–10 minutes on each side and garnish with cilantro. Serve with soba noodles and stir-fried oyster mushrooms.

For sesame greens with black bean sauce, to accompany the chicken, fry 2 tablespoons sesame seeds in 1 teaspoon sunflower oil until lightly browned. Add 1 tablespoon soy sauce, cover with a lid and take off the heat. When the bubbling subsides, scoop the seeds into a dish. Rinse 13 oz collard greens and thickly slice, stir fry in 1 tablespoon oil with 2 finely chopped garlic cloves until just wilted. Mix in 3 tablespoons ready-made black bean sauce. Serve sprinkled with the seeds.

polenta crusted chicken strips

Serves **4**
Preparation time **20 minutes**
Cooking time **15 minutes**

1½ cups **instant polenta grains**

8 tablespoons ready-grated **Parmesan cheese**

2 **eggs**

4 boneless, skinless **chicken breasts**, cut into slices of even thickness

2 oz **sundried tomatoes in oil**, sliced

10 oz **cherry tomatoes**, halved

3 tablespoons **olive oil**

2 teaspoons **green pesto**

3⅓ cups **water**

½ cup **heavy cream**

tiny **basil leaves**, to garnish (optional)

salt and **pepper**

Mix ⅓ cup polenta on a plate with 2 tablespoons of Parmesan. Beat the eggs in a shallow dish. Dip the chicken slices into the egg, then roll in the polenta mix until thinly coated. Put on a plate and set aside.

Put the sundried tomatoes into a shallow ovenproof dish, then put the fresh tomatoes on top, add 1 tablespoon oil, the pesto, and a little seasoning. Broil for 5 minutes.

Bring the measured water to a boil in a nonstick saucepan, add the remaining polenta, bring back to a boil and stir constantly until thickened and smooth. Mix in the remaining Parmesan and season generously. Set aside.

Heat the remaining oil in a skillet, add the chicken and fry for 8–10 minutes, turning until golden and cooked through. Reheat the soft polenta, gradually mixing in the cream and a little extra water if needed, until soft.

Spoon the polenta onto plates, top with the tomatoes, then arrange the chicken strips on top. Garnish with basil leaves, if desired.

For chicken strips with garlicky tomato sauce,
make up the chicken as above but coating in 2 cups fresh bread crumbs mixed with 2 tablespoons Parmesan instead of the polenta. Cook as above. Meanwhile, fry 1 chopped onion in 1 tablespoon olive oil until softened. Add 2 finely chopped garlic cloves, a 13 oz can chopped tomatoes, 1 teaspoon superfine sugar, and seasoning. Simmer for 5 minutes. Serve with the chicken and chunky oven fries.

asian chicken cakes

Serves **4**

Preparation time **15 minutes**

Cooking time **16 minutes**

1 lb 3 oz **ground chicken**

1 stalk **lemon grass**, very finely chopped

2 **kaffir lime leaves**, very finely chopped

2 inch piece **ginger root**, peeled, very finely chopped

2 **green chilies**, very finely chopped

2 **garlic cloves**, very finely chopped

1 **egg**, beaten

1 tablespoon **sesame seeds**, toasted

chili and ginger jam (see page 174), to serve

Place the chicken in a large bowl with the lemon grass, kaffir lime leaves, ginger, chili, and garlic, which need to be so finely chopped as to almost make a paste. Add the beaten egg and sesame seeds. Mix well, using your hands.

Heat a griddle pan (or ordinary skillet). Divide the mixture into 24 and shape into small patties. Cook for 8 minutes on each side.

Serve the chicken cakes with chili and ginger jam (see page 174), a salad of rice noodles, chopped peanuts, sliced onion, bean sprouts, and lots of chopped cilantro.

For Chinese cabbage & bean sprout salad,

as an alternative salad accompaniment, mix 4 tablespoons sunflower oil, 2 tablespoons rice vinegar, 2 tablespoons light soy sauce, and 2 teaspoons fish sauce in a bowl. Add 6 cups sliced Chinese cabbage, 1½ cups rinsed and drained bean sprouts, 4 sliced scallions, 8 oz carrots cut into matchstick strips, ⅓ cup roughly chopped salted peanuts, and 2 tablespoons chopped mint, then toss together.

thai chicken satay

Serves **4**

Preparation time **30 minutes**,
plus marinating

Cooking time **16 minutes**

4 boneless, skinless **chicken
breasts**, cut into thin slices

2 **garlic cloves**, finely chopped

1½ inch piece **ginger root**,
peeled and grated

2 tablespoons **light soy sauce**

2 tablespoons **lemon juice**

1 tablespoon **sunflower oil**

2 **shallots** or ½ **onion**,
finely sliced

1 **garlic clove**, finely sliced

1 small hot **Thai chili**,
thinly sliced

1 inch piece **ginger root**,
peeled and grated

4 tablespoons **crunchy
peanut butter**

¾ cup canned **low-fat
coconut milk**

2 teaspoons **fish sauce**

1 tablespoon **light soy sauce**

Mix the chicken with the garlic, ginger, light soy sauce, and lemon juice and then allow to stand for 30 minutes.

Heat the sunflower oil in a small saucepan. Add the shallots or onion and fry gently until softened but not brown. Mix in the garlic, chili, and second batch of ginger and cook for 1 minute before adding all the remaining ingredients. Simmer gently for 5 minutes.

Thread the marinated chicken slices in a zigzag pattern onto 12 thin metal skewers. Cook under a hot broiler for 10 minutes, turning once or twice until the chicken is browned and cooked through. Garnish with lime wedges and serve with rice and a salad.

For pickled Thai cucumber salad, to serve with the chicken satay, heat 4 tablespoons rice vinegar in a saucepan with 4 tablespoons superfine sugar and ½–1 thinly sliced hot Thai red chili to taste. When the sugar has dissolved, boil for 1 minute. Add ½ a thinly sliced cucumber and allow to cool.

asian 5-spice glazed chicken

Serves **4**
Preparation time **20 minutes**
Cooking time **40–45 minutes**

2 **red onions**, cut into wedges
2 tablespoon **sunflower oil**
4 **chicken thighs**
4 **chicken drumsticks**
4 **red plums**, halved, pitted
3 tablespoons **red currant jelly**
1 tablespoon **red wine vinegar**
2 tablespoons **dark soy sauce**
½ teaspoon **5-spice powder**
⅔ cup **water**
4 oz **bok choy**

Toss the onion wedges in 1 tablespoon of the oil in a large roasting pan. Slash each chicken joint 2–3 times with a knife, then add to the roasting pan with the plums.

Warm the red currant jelly, vinegar, soy sauce, and 5-spice in a small saucepan until the jelly has melted, then brush liberally over the chicken, reserving about one-third for later. Pour the measured water into the base of the pan, avoiding the chicken, so that the glaze will not burn on the bottom of the pan.

Roast, uncovered in a preheated oven, 375°F, for 40–45 minutes, brushing with the remaining glaze once during cooking. Test the chicken (see page 11).

Heat the remaining oil in a skillet and add the bok choy. Fry for 2–3 minutes until tender and then add to the roasting pan just before serving.

Spoon onto plates and serve with rice.

For balsamic glazed chicken, toss the onions in 1 tablespoon olive oil, then add the chicken as above but with 9 oz Chantenay carrots instead of the plums. Mix 3 tablespoons balsamic vinegar with 3 tablespoons white wine, 1 tablespoon olive oil, and 1 tablespoon honey, then brush this over the chicken in place of the red currant glaze, tucking 4 bay leaves in between the joints. Roast as above with the water.

griddled chicken burgers

Serves **4**
Preparation time **20 minutes**
Cooking time **12–20 minutes**

1¼ lb **ground chicken**
1 **shallot**, finely chopped
small bunch **thyme**, chopped,
  plus extra to garnish
  (optional)
1 teaspoon **Worcestershire
  sauce**
3 drops **Tabasco sauce**
2 **egg yolks**
1 **ciabatta loaf**
Dijon mustard, for spreading
mayonnaise, for spreading
2 **tomatoes**, sliced
1 bag **herb salad leaves**
salt and **pepper**

Place the chicken in a large bowl. Add the shallot, thyme, Worcestershire and Tabasco sauces, and egg yolks. Season to taste and mix well.

Heat a griddle pan (or ordinary skillet). Using your hands, divide the chicken mixture into 4. Shape into patties and cook for 6–10 minutes on each side, depending on the thickness of the patties.

Cut the ciabatta in half horizontally and toast the 2 lengths under a preheated broiler. Cut each piece in half. Spread the ciabatta with mustard and mayonnaise. Top with tomato slices and herb salad leaves, finally adding the griddled chicken burgers on top. Garnish with a little chopped thyme, if desired.

For Mediterranean burgers, omit the Worcestershire sauce and stir in ½ cup each of pitted and chopped black olives and sundried tomatoes, drained of their oil. Shape, cook, and serve as above, minus the mustard.

creamy chicken gnocchi

Serves **4**
Preparation time **15 minutes**
Cooking time **14–16 minutes**

2 tablespoons **olive oil**
1 **onion**, thinly sliced
1 lb **butternut squash**,
  peeled, seeded, cut into
  small dice
4 slices **bacon**, diced
14 oz **mini chicken breast
  fillets**, diced
12 **sage leaves**
1¼ cups **chicken stock**
  (see page 10)
1 lb pack **chilled gnocchi**
6 tablespoons **sour cream**
4 tablespoons freshly grated
  Parmesan cheese
salt and **pepper**

Heat the oil in a skillet, add the onion, butternut squash, and bacon and fry for 5 minutes until just beginning to brown. Stir in the chicken and sage and fry for 5 minutes, stirring until golden.

Add the stock and a little seasoning and cook for 2–3 minutes until the chicken and squash are cooked through.

Bring a large saucepan of water to a boil, add the gnocchi, and cook for 2–3 minutes until the gnocchi rise to the surface. Drain and add to the skillet with the sour cream. Gently toss together, then spoon into shallow bowls and sprinkle with the Parmesan.

For chicken, butternut squash, & sage risotto, mix 1 cup risotto rice into the fried-chicken mixture, then stir in ⅔ cup dry white wine and 4 cups hot chicken stock (see page 10), in three batches, topping up as the rice absorbs the liquid. Simmer uncovered for 20 minutes, stirring occasionally until the rice is soft. Spoon into bowls and sprinkle with Parmesan.

blackened chicken & beans

Serves **4**
Preparation time **30 minutes**
Cooking time **40 minutes**

4 **chicken thighs**
4 **chicken drumsticks**
1 teaspoon **cumin seeds**
1 teaspoon **fennel seeds**
1 teaspoon **dried thyme
leaves**
¼ teaspoon **ground cinnamon**
½ teaspoon **smoked paprika**
1 tablespoon **sunflower oil**
1 tablespoon **tomato paste**
1 tablespoon **vinegar**
2 tablespoons **dark brown
sugar**
2 tablespoons **pineapple
juice** (from can below)

For the black-eye bean salad
7½ oz can **pineapple in juice**,
juice reserved, pineapple
chopped
13½ oz can **black-eye beans**,
drained
small bunch **cilantro**, roughly
chopped
½ **red onion**, finely chopped
1 **red bell pepper**, cored,
seeded, diced
grated zest and juice of 1 **lime**

Slash the chicken joints 2–3 times with a knife, then
put into a roasting pan. Roughly crush the seeds
then mix with the next 8 ingredients and spoon
over the chicken.

Add 4 tablespoons water to the base of the roasting
pan, then bake the chicken in a preheated oven, 350°F,
for 40 minutes, spooning pan juices over once or twice
until the chicken is deep brown in color and the juices
run clear when the chicken is tested (see page 11).

Meanwhile, to make the bean salad, pour the
remaining canned pineapple juice into a bowl and
add the chopped pineapple and all the remaining
ingredients. Mix together, then serve spoonfuls with
the cooked chicken.

For blackened chicken with rice & peas, bake
the chicken as above but omit the black-eye bean
salad. Bring 4 cups chicken stock (see page 10)
and 1¾ cups can low-fat coconut milk to a boil in
a saucepan. Add 1 cup long-grain white rice that
has been rinsed with cold water and drained, and
a 13½ oz can drained red kidney beans. Simmer for
8 minutes, add ¾ cup frozen peas, and top up with
extra boiling water. Cook for 2 minutes, then serve
with the chicken.

thai sesame chicken patties

Serves **4**
Preparation time **15 minutes**,
  plus chilling
Cooking time **10 minutes**

4 scallions
¼ cup **cilantro**, plus extra
  to garnish
1 lb **ground chicken**
3 tablespoons **sesame
  seeds**, toasted
1 tablespoon **light soy sauce**
1½ inch piece **ginger root**,
  finely grated
1 **egg white**
1 tablespoon **sesame oil**
1 tablespoon **sunflower oil**
**Thai sweet chili dipping
  sauce**, to serve
scallion curls, to garnish
  (optional)

Finely chop the scallions and cilantro in a food processor or with a knife. Mix with the chicken, sesame seeds, soy sauce, ginger, and egg white.

Divide the mixture into 20 mounds on a cutting board, then shape into slightly flattened rounds with wetted hands. Chill for 1 hour (or longer if you have time).

Heat the sesame and sunflower oils in a large skillet, add the patties and fry for 10 minutes, turning once or twice until golden and cooked through to the center. Arrange on a serving plate with a small bowl of chili dipping sauce in the center. Garnish with extra cilantro leaves and scallion curls, if desired.

For baby leaf stir-fry with chili to serve as an accompaniment, heat 2 teaspoons sesame oil in the finished pattie pan, add an 8 oz pack of ready-prepared baby leaf and baby vegetable stir-fry ingredients and stir-fry for 2–3 minutes until the vegetables are hot. Mix in 2 tablespoons light soy sauce and 1 tablespoon Thai sweet chili dipping sauce. Serve in a side bowl with the chicken patties.

stoved chicken with black pudding

Serves **4**
Preparation time **20 minutes**
Cooking time **2 hours
5 minutes**

4 **chicken thigh** and
   drumstick joints
2 tablespoons **all-purpose
   flour**
1 tablespoon **sunflower oil**
2 **onions**, thinly sliced
¼ cup **butter**
2 lb **potatoes**, thinly sliced
1 **dessert apple**, cored, diced
4 oz **black pudding**, peeled,
   diced
1¾ cups **chicken stock**
   (see page 10)
salt and **pepper**

Coat the chicken in the flour and seasoning.

Heat the oil in a large skillet, add the onions,
and fry for 5 minutes until pale golden. Mix in any
remaining flour, then scoop the onions out of the
pan and set aside.

Heat half the butter in the skillet, add the chicken and
fry on both sides until golden. Arrange a thin layer of
potatoes in the base of an ovenproof casserole dish,
top with half the onions, then the chicken pieces. Add
the apple and black pudding, then spoon over the
remaining onions. Arrange the remaining potatoes in
an overlapping layer on the top. Pour the stock over
the top, then season the potatoes.

Cover the dish tightly and cook in a preheated oven,
350°F, for 1½ hours. Remove the lid, dot the potatoes
with the remaining butter and cook for 30 minutes
more until golden brown. Serve in shallow bowls.

For stoved chicken with bacon & sage, omit the
black pudding and apple and add 4 oz diced bacon
when frying the onions. Add 2–3 stems sage,
depending on size, to the casserole dish along
with the fried chicken.

italian pesto chicken burgers

Serves **4**

Preparation time **15 minutes**, plus chilling

Cooking time **10–13 minutes**

1 lb **ground chicken**

2 **garlic cloves**, finely chopped

4 **scallions**, finely chopped

2 teaspoons **pesto**

1 **egg yolk**

1 tablespoon **sunflower oil**

4 **ciabatta rolls**

2 tablespoons **mayonnaise**

1 cup **arugula, watercress, and spinach salad**

2 oz **sundried tomatoes in oil**, drained, sliced

salt and **pepper**

Put the chicken, garlic, scallions, pesto, and egg yolk in a bowl, add seasoning, then mix together well. Divide into 4, then shape into thick burgers. Chill for 1 hour.

Heat the oil in a nonstick skillet, add the burgers and fry for about 10–13 minutes, turning once or twice until golden brown and cooked through.

Split the ciabatta rolls in half and lightly toast the cut sides. Spread with mayonnaise, then add the salad and tomatoes to the lower half of each roll. Top with the burgers and the other half of each roll, and serve with oven fries.

For curried chicken burgers, mix 2 teaspoons hot curry paste and 2 tablespoons chopped cilantro into the chicken mixture instead of the pesto. Fry as above, then serve in warmed round naan breads with salad and mango chutney.

chicken tikka masala

Serves **4**

Preparation time **20 minutes**

Cooking time **20 minutes**

2 tablespoons **butter**

4 boneless, skinless **chicken breasts**, cubed

1 **onion**, quartered

1½ inch piece **ginger root**, sliced

3 **garlic cloves**, sliced

1 **hot red chili**, sliced, including seeds

1 teaspoon **cumin seeds**, roughly crushed

1 teaspoon **coriander seeds**, roughly crushed

1 teaspoon **turmeric**

1 teaspoon **paprika**

2 teaspoons **garam masala**

1¼ cups **chicken stock** (see page 10)

⅔ cup **heavy cream**

4 tablespoons **cilantro**, chopped, plus extra to garnish

juice of ½–1 lemon

Heat the butter in a saucepan, add the chicken and fry for 3 minutes. Finely chop the onion, ginger, garlic, and chili in a food processor or with a knife. Add to the chicken and fry for 5 minutes, stirring until lightly browned.

Mix in the spices and cook for 3–4 minutes until well browned. Stir in the stock and cream, then simmer for 10 minutes, stirring occasionally until the chicken is tender.

Stir in the chopped cilantro and lemon juice to taste. Cook for 1 minute, then garnish with extra cilantro. Serve with rice and naan bread.

For chicken tikka, mix the diced chicken breast with the juice of ½ lemon and ¼ teaspoon salt. Mix ⅔ cup plain yogurt with 1½ inch grated ginger root, 3 finely chopped garlic cloves, and 1 finely chopped red chili. Stir in the spices as above and add 4 tablespoons sunflower oil. Marinate in the refrigerator overnight. Spoon the chicken onto a foil-lined baking sheet and cook in a preheated oven, 425°F, for 15 minutes, turning the chicken and brushing with the remaining marinade halfway through cooking. Serve with salad.

chicken balti with whole spices

Serves **4**
Preparation time **20 minutes**
Cooking time **38–41 minutes**

1 **onion**, quartered
1 inch piece **ginger root**, sliced
3 **garlic cloves**
2 tablespoons **sunflower oil**
8 boneless, skinless **chicken thighs**, cut into cubes
1 teaspoon **cumin seeds**, roughly crushed
1 **cinnamon stick**, halved
8 **cardamom pods**, roughly crushed
6 **cloves**
½ teaspoon **turmeric**
1 teaspoon **dried red pepper flakes**
13 oz can **chopped tomatoes**
2½ cups **chicken stock** (see page 10)
small bunch **cilantro**
¼ cup **slivered almonds**, toasted, to garnish

Finely chop the onion, ginger, and garlic in a food processor or with a large knife. Heat the oil in a medium saucepan, add the chicken and fry for 5 minutes, stirring until lightly browned. Stir in the chopped onion mix and fry for 2–3 minutes until softened.

Stir in the spices and pepper flakes and cook for 1 minute, then mix in the tomatoes and stock. Bring to a boil, then cover and simmer for 30 minutes, stirring occasionally.

Tear the cilantro into pieces, add to the balti and cook for 1 minute, then spoon into bowls. Garnishing with the toasted almonds, serve with rice and naan bread.

For chicken balti with mushrooms & spinach, omit the seeds, cardamom, cloves, turmeric, and pepper flakes and stir in 2 tablespoons medium hot balti curry paste instead. Mix in 1¼ cups sliced cup mushrooms and cook as above. Stir in 3 cups baby leaf spinach along with the cilantro at the end and cook until the spinach has just wilted.

maple glazed chicken

Serves **4**
Preparation time **15 minutes**
Cooking time **40–45 minutes**

4 **chicken thigh** and
  drumstick joints
2 **dessert apples**, cored,
  quartered
8 oz **shallots**, peeled, halved
  if large
1¼ lb **parsnips**, quartered
6 **bay leaves**
2 tablespoons **olive oil**
2 tablespoons **maple syrup**
2 tablespoons **cider vinegar**
salt and **pepper**

Slash the chicken joints 3–4 times, then put them into a large roasting pan with the apples, shallots, parsnips, and bay leaves.

Mix the remaining ingredients together and spoon over the chicken and vegetables. Add 4 tablespoons water to the base of the pan. Cook in a preheated oven, 375°F, for 40–45 minutes, spooning the glaze over the chicken once or twice until deep brown and cooked through when tested (see page 11).

Spoon onto plates and serve with an arugula salad.

For mango chutney-glazed chicken, add 1 small mango, peeled, pitted, and cut into thick slices instead of the apple. Omit the maple syrup and mix 2 tablespoons mango chutney with the oil and vinegar mix. Cook as above. Mix ⅔ cup plain yogurt with 3 tablespoons chopped cilantro and an extra tablespoon of mango chutney. Serve spoonfuls with the chicken.

chicken, bacon, & sage meatballs

Serves **4**

Preparation time **30 minutes**,
plus chilling

Cooking time **20 minutes**

4 oz **cup mushrooms**, finely
chopped

2 slices **bacon**, chopped

1 lb **ground chicken**

2 tablespoons **sage**, finely
chopped

1 **egg yolk**

2 tablespoons **sunflower oil**

2 **onions**, thinly sliced

2 teaspoons **superfine sugar**

2 tablespoons **all-purpose
flour**

1¾ cups **chicken stock**
(see page 10)

salt and **pepper**

Mix the mushrooms and bacon with the chicken, then stir in the sage, egg yolk, and seasoning. Shape into 20 small meatballs and chill for 30 minutes.

Fry the meatballs in 1 tablespoon of the oil for 5 minutes until lightly browned all over, then transfer to a roasting pan and cook in a preheated oven, 375°F, for 15 minutes.

Meanwhile, fry the onions in the remaining oil in the cleaned skillet until softened and just beginning to brown. Sprinkle with the sugar and cook for 5 minutes more, stirring frequently until a deep brown.

Mix in the flour, then gradually mix in the stock, season, and bring to a boil. Simmer for 2–3 minutes until thickened. Add the meatballs to the gravy and gently stir. Spoon into bowls and serve with mashed potatoes, peas, and green beans.

For chicken meatballs with mustard sauce, oven-bake the meatballs as above. Wash and dry the skillet, then fry 1 chopped onion in ¼ cup butter until softened but not browned. Stir in 6 tablespoons all-purpose flour, then gradually mix in 1¾ cups chicken stock (see page 10). Stir in 3 teaspoons mild Dijon or Swedish mustard, ½ teaspoon turmeric, and seasoning. Simmer and finish as above.

chicken thatch

Serves **4**
Preparation time **25 minutes**
Cooking time **35 minutes**

1 tablespoon **sunflower oil**
4 boneless, skinless **chicken thighs**, diced
1 **onion**, chopped
2 tablespoons **all-purpose flour**
1¾ cups **chicken stock** (see page 10)
2 teaspoons **Dijon mustard**
1 large **carrot**, diced
1½ lb **potatoes**, quartered
1 **zucchini**, diced
1 cup **sugar snap peas**, halved
½ cup **frozen peas**
3 tablespoons **butter**
3 tablespoons **milk**
¾ cup grated **mature cheddar cheese**
salt and **pepper**

Heat the oil in a saucepan, add the chicken and onion and fry for 5 minutes, stirring until browned. Stir in the flour, then gradually mix in the stock. Bring to a boil, then add the mustard, carrot, and a little seasoning. Cover and simmer for 30 minutes.

Meanwhile, cook the potatoes in a saucepan of boiling water until tender. Add the zucchini, sugar snap peas, and frozen peas to a smaller saucepan of boiling water and cook for 3 minutes. Drain and set aside.

Drain the potatoes and mash with two-thirds of the butter and all the milk. Season and stir in two-thirds of the cheese.

Spoon the chicken mixture into a 5 cup pie dish or 4 individual dishes, add the just-cooked green vegetables, then spoon the mash on top. Dot with the remaining butter and sprinkle with the remaining cheese. Broil until golden, then serve immediately. (For an oven-baked chicken thatch, chill the dish once the grated cheese has been sprinkled on top, then bake when needed, in a preheated oven, 375°F, for 35 minutes until piping hot or 25 minutes for smaller dishes.)

For chicken & bacon thatch, add 4 chopped slices of Canadian bacon when frying the chicken and onion. Omit the zucchini, sugar snaps, and peas and cook ½ cup frozen corn instead. Drain and add to the chicken. Finish as above.

chicken liver & pancetta ragu

Serves **4**
Preparation time **15 minutes**
Cooking time **16–17 minutes**

13 oz **tagliatelle**
1 tablespoon **olive oil**
4 boneless, skinless **chicken thighs**, diced
1 **onion**, chopped
3 oz **pancetta**, diced
4 oz **chicken livers**, defrosted if frozen, well rinsed
2 **garlic cloves**, finely chopped
⅔ cup **red wine**
½ cup **chicken stock** (see page 10)
4 teaspoons **sundried tomato paste**
small bunch **basil**
Parmesan cheese, grated, to garnish
salt and **pepper**

Bring a large saucepan of water to a boil, add the tagliatelle and cook for 8–10 minutes until just tender, then drain into a colander.

Meanwhile, heat the oil in a large skillet, add the chicken, onion, and pancetta and fry for 10 minutes, stirring until golden. Chop the chicken livers, discarding any white cores, then add to the pan with the garlic and fry for 3 minutes.

Stir in the red wine, stock, and tomato paste, then a little seasoning. Cook over a high heat for 3–4 minutes until the sauce is reduced slightly. Tear half the basil leaves into pieces and add to the chicken, then cook for 1 minute.

Stir the tagliatelle into the chicken mixture and reheat if needed. Spoon into shallow bowls and sprinkle with the remaining basil leaves and grated Parmesan.

For chicken & walnut ragu, omit the chicken livers and use ⅓ cup roughly chopped walnut pieces instead. Toss with chopped parsley and sprinkle with extra parsley to garnish.

chicken maryland & banana fritters

Serves **4**
Preparation time **25 minutes**
Cooking time **20 minutes**

½ cup **all-purpose flour**
¼ teaspoon each **powdered mustard, turmeric,** and **cayenne pepper**
8 **chicken drumsticks**
4 tablespoons **milk**
4 tablespoons **sunflower oil**
1 cup **frozen corn**
4 tablespoons **heavy cream**
4 tablespoons **water**
4 **scallions**, chopped
1 **red bell pepper**, cored, seeded, diced
parsley, chopped, to garnish (optional)
salt

For the banana fritters
1 small ripe **banana**
1 cup **self-rising flour**
2 **eggs**
½ teaspoon **dried red pepper flakes**
⅔ cup **milk**
salt and **pepper**

Mix the flour, mustard, turmeric, cayenne, and a pinch of salt on a plate. Dip the chicken in the milk, then coat thickly in the flour and spice mixture.

Heat 3 tablespoons of the oil in a skillet, add the chicken and fry, turning, until golden all over. Transfer to a roasting pan and cook in a preheated oven, 400°F, for 20 minutes or until the chicken is cooked through when tested (see page 11).

Meanwhile, put the corn, cream, water, scallions, and red pepper into a saucepan, cover, and simmer for 5 minutes until hot, then set aside.

Make the fritters by mashing the banana on a plate, then putting it into a bowl with the flour, eggs, pepper flakes, and seasoning. Gradually beat in the milk until smooth. Heat the remaining oil in the cleaned skillet, add dessertspoonfuls of the fritter mixture and fry over a moderate heat until bubbles appear on the surface and the undersides are golden. Turn over and cook the second side until golden. Keep hot.

Reheat the corn mixture, then spoon into small bowls set on dinner plates, add the chicken and fritters to the plates and garnish with chopped parsley, if desired.

For chicken Maryland with fried bananas & bacon, bake the chicken as above. Simmer 4 halved corn ears in a pan of water for 15 minutes until tender. Wash and dry the chicken pan, then fry 2 thickly sliced bananas and 6 slices of bacon in 1 tablespoon sunflower oil until golden. Cut the bacon into thin strips and arrange on a serving plate with the chicken, corn ears, and bananas.

caribbean chicken skewers & salsa

Serves **4**
Preparation time **30 minutes**,
  plus marinating
Cooking time **35–42 minutes**

4 tablespoons **pineapple
  juice** (from can below)
1 tablespoon **tomato ketchup**
1 teaspoon **paprika**
½ teaspoon **ground cinnamon**
large pinch **ground allspice**
4 boneless, skinless **chicken
  breasts**, cubed
1 **red bell pepper**, cored,
  seeded, cut into chunks
1 **orange bell pepper**, cored,
  seeded, cut into chunks

For the salsa
7½ oz can **pineapple rings in
  natural juice**, drained
2 **tomatoes**, diced
½ cup **frozen corn**, just
  thawed
½ **red chili**, seeded, finely
  chopped (optional)
¾ inch piece **ginger root**,
  finely chopped
small bunch **cilantro**, roughly
  chopped

Put the pineapple juice into a bowl. Stir the ketchup and spices into the juice, add the chicken and toss together. Allow to marinate for at least 30 minutes.

Meanwhile, to make the salsa, finely chop the pineapple rings and put in a bowl with the tomatoes and corn. Add the chili (if using), ginger, and half the cilantro and toss together.

Thread the pepper chunks onto 12 wooden or metal skewers, alternating with the chicken pieces. Sprinkle the skewers with the remaining chopped cilantro. Broil the skewers under a preheated hot broiler for 10–12 minutes, turning several times until well browned and the chicken is cooked through.

Serve the skewers with brown rice and spoonfuls of the salsa.

For Caribbean rice salad, as an accompaniment to the skewers, put 1 cup easy-cook brown rice in a saucepan of boiling water and cook for 25–30 minutes or until tender. Drain the rice, rinse well with cold water then drain again. Mix it with the salsa, 5–7 oz diced cooked chicken, 4 tablespoons toasted shredded coconut, and 1 seeded and diced red bell pepper.

peppered chicken & eggplant

Serves **4**
Preparation time **15 minutes**
Cooking time **15 minutes**

2 tablespoons **sunflower oil**
6 boneless, skinless **chicken thighs,** cut into cubes
1 large **eggplant**, diced
1 **red onion**, sliced
2 **garlic cloves**, finely chopped
2 tablespoons **medium hot curry paste**
½ teaspoon **black peppercorns**, roughly crushed
small bunch **cilantro**, to garnish

Heat the oil in a large skillet, add the chicken and eggplant and fry, stirring for 5 minutes until the eggplant is just beginning to soften. Stir in the onion and garlic and fry for 5 more minutes, stirring until the onion and chicken are just beginning to brown.

Mix in the curry paste and peppercorns and fry for 5 minutes until the chicken is a rich golden brown and cooked through when tested (see page 11). Tear the cilantro into pieces and sprinkle over the top. Serve immediately with bowls of tomato salad, yogurt, and rice.

For curried chicken with mixed vegetables, use a small eggplant rather than a large one, then mix in 1 diced zucchini and 1 diced and seeded green bell pepper along with the onion. Finish with 2 cups spinach and cook for 2 minutes until just wilted.

penne with chicken livers

Serves **4**
Preparation time **10 minutes**
Cooking time **10–15 minutes**

1 **yellow bell pepper**, cored, seeded
10 oz **penne**
1 tablespoon **olive oil**
2 tablespoons **butter**
1 **red onion**, sliced
8 oz **chicken livers**, trimmed
1 **rosemary sprig**, chopped
salt and **pepper**
¼ cup grated **Parmesan cheese**, to serve

Roast the yellow pepper in a hot oven or under a preheated hot broiler, skin-side up, until the skin is blistered and black. Place in a plastic bag and allow to cool, then peel off the skin. Cut the flesh into strips.

Cook the penne in lightly salted boiling water, according to the package instructions.

Meanwhile, heat the oil and butter in a large skillet, add the sliced onion and chicken livers and cook over a high heat until browned all over. Add the rosemary, the strips of yellow pepper, and seasoning. Do not overcook the livers as they will become dry and hard—they are best when still pink in the middle.

Mix the chicken liver mixture with the cooked pasta and toss well. Serve immediately with the Parmesan.

For chicken-liver crostini, make up the liver mixture as above but cut the pepper and onion into dice rather than slices. Instead of tossing the liver mixture with pasta, spoon it onto toasted slices of ciabatta bread that have been rubbed with a cut clove of garlic and drizzled with a little oil. Sprinkle with Parmesan shavings and serve warm or cold.

food for
friends

spiced chicken with yogurt crust

Serves **4**
Preparation time **30 minutes**,
  plus marinating
Cooking time **1 hour**
  20 minutes

3 lb **whole chicken**
1 inch piece **ginger root**,
  sliced
2 small **green chilies**
small bunch **cilantro**, plus
  extra to garnish
4 **garlic cloves**, peeled
¾ cup **low-fat plain yogurt**
grated zest and juice of
  1 **lemon**
1 teaspoon each **ground
  garam masala** and **ground
  turmeric**
1 teaspoon **cumin seeds**,
  roughly crushed
1 teaspoon **salt**
¼ cup **butter**, melted

Slash each chicken leg and breast 2–3 times with a sharp knife, then put the chicken in a large plastic bag. Finely chop the ginger, chilies, cilantro, and garlic in a food processor or with a large knife. Mix into the yogurt, then stir in the lemon zest and juice, spices, and salt. Spoon the mixture into the plastic bag, seal well and refrigerate for 4 hours (or overnight).

Allow the chicken to come to room temperature for 1 hour, then remove it from the bag (with a thick coating) and put it in a roasting pan. Spoon 4 tablespoons of water into the base of the pan. Drizzle the chicken with butter.

Roast, uncovered, in a preheated oven, 375°F, for 1 hour 20 minutes, spooning a little more of the yogurt marinade over the chicken once or twice.

Test the chicken (see page 11). When cooked through, transfer it to a serving dish, garnish with cilantro and serve with pilau rice.

For nectarine chutney, as an accompaniment, fry 1 finely chopped red onion in 1 tablespoon of sunflower oil for 5 minutes. Add 6 roughly crushed cardamom pods, then mix in 13 oz nectarines and 2 tablespoons each of red wine vinegar, light brown sugar, and water. Cover and simmer for 10 minutes.

classic coq au vin

Serves **4**

Preparation time **25 minutes**

Cooking time **1 hour
20 minutes**

2 tablespoons **all-purpose
flour**

8 mixed **chicken thigh** and
drumstick joints

2 tablespoons **olive oil**

12 oz **shallots,** halved if large

4 oz **bacon**

2 **garlic cloves**, finely chopped

4 tablespoons **brandy** or
cognac

1¼ cups **cheap burgundy
red wine**

¾ cup **chicken stock**
(see page 10)

2 teaspoons **tomato paste**

fresh or dried **bouquet garni**

salt and **pepper**

For the garlic croutons

2 tablespoons **butter**

1 tablespoon **olive oil**

1 **garlic clove**, finely chopped

½ stick **French bread**, thinly
sliced

Mix the flour on a plate with a little seasoning, then use to coat the chicken joints. Heat the oil in a large shallow flameproof casserole (or skillet and transfer chicken to a casserole dish later), add the chicken, and cook over a high heat until golden on all sides. Lift out onto a plate.

Fry the shallots and bacon until golden, then stir in the garlic and return the chicken to the casserole. Pour over the brandy or cognac and when bubbling flame with a long taper. As soon as the flames subside, pour in the red wine and stock, then mix in the tomato paste and bouquet garni. Season, then cover the casserole and transfer to a preheated oven, 350°F, and cook for 1¼ hours until tender.

When the chicken is cooked, pour the liquid from the casserole into a saucepan and boil for 5 minutes to reduce and thicken slightly, if desired. Return the liquid to the casserole.

Heat the butter and oil in a skillet for the croutons, add the garlic, and cook for 1 minute, then add the bread slices in a single layer. Fry on both sides until golden. Serve the coq au vin in shallow bowls topped with the croutons.

For flamed chicken with calvados & apple, fry the chicken as above, adding 4 tablespoons calvados instead of the brandy. Pour in 1¼ cups hard cider in place of the red wine and omit the tomato paste. Transfer to a casserole dish and add 1 cored and thickly sliced Granny Smith dessert apple. Continue as above.

chicken with preserved lemons

Serves **4–5**
Preparation time **20 minutes**
Cooking time **1 hour
45 minutes**

2 tablespoons **olive oil**
1 **onion**, finely chopped
3 **garlic cloves**
1 teaspoon **ground ginger**
1½ teaspoons **ground
cinnamon**
large pinch **saffron threads**,
toasted, crushed
3½ lb **whole chicken**
3 cups **chicken stock**
(see page 10) or water
1 cup large **black olives**,
rinsed, soaked (optional)
1 **preserved lemon**, chopped
large bunch **cilantro**, finely
chopped
large bunch **parsley**, finely
chopped
salt and **pepper**

Heat the oil in a skillet, add the onion and fry gently,
stirring frequently until softened and golden.

Meanwhile, using a mortar and pestle, crush the garlic
with a pinch of salt, then work in the ginger, cinnamon,
saffron, and a little pepper. Stir into the onions, cook
until fragrant, then remove from the pan and spread
over the chicken.

Put the chicken into a heavy saucepan or flameproof
casserole that it just fits, heat gently, and brown the
chicken for about 2–3 minutes, turning often. Add the
stock or water, and bring to just simmering point. Cover
and simmer gently for about 1¼ hours, turning the
chicken over 2–3 times.

Add the olives, preserved lemon, cilantro, and parsley
to the pan. Cover and cook for about 15 minutes until
the chicken is very tender. Taste the sauce—if the flavor
needs to be more concentrated, transfer the chicken to
a warmed serving dish, cover and keep warm, and boil
the cooking juices to a rich sauce. Tilt the pan and
skim off any surplus fat, then pour over the chicken.
Serve with couscous, if desired.

For chicken & tomato tagine, reduce the stock or
water to 1¾ cups and add a 13 oz can of chopped
tomatoes. Cover and simmer as above. Omit the
olives and lemon instead adding ½ cup thickly sliced
okra and the cilantro and parsley as above for the last
5 minutes of cooking. Serve with rice or warmed Arab
flat breads.

chicken with 30 garlic cloves

Serves **4**
Preparation time **25 minutes**
Cooking time **1 hour**
   30 minutes

4 **chicken leg** and **thigh
   joints**
2 tablespoons **butter**
1 tablespoon **olive oil**
8 oz **shallots**, halved if large
2 tablespoons **all-purpose
   flour**
¾ cup **dry white wine**
¾ cup **chicken stock**
   (see page 10)
2 teaspoons **Dijon mustard**
3 **garlic bulbs**
small bunch **thyme**
4 tablespoons **sour cream**,
   optional
salt and **pepper**

Fry the chicken in the butter and oil in a skillet, until golden on both sides. Transfer to a large casserole dish.

Fry the shallots until softened and lightly browned. Stir in the flour, then gradually mix in the wine, stock, mustard, and seasoning. Bring to a boil, stirring.

Separate the garlic cloves but do not peel them. Count out 30 cloves and add to the casserole dish with 3–4 thyme stems. Pour over the wine mix, then cover and cook in a preheated oven, 350°F, for 1½ hours.

Stir in the sour cream, if desired, and serve with mashed potatoes and green beans.

For baked chicken with flageolet beans & parsley, fry the chicken and onion as above with just 2 finely chopped garlic cloves added to the onion. Mix with the wine, stock, mustard, and seasoning, then add a 13 oz can drained flageolet beans to the casserole with the thyme. Remove the thyme at the end and stir in 4 tablespoons chopped parsley, omitting the sour cream.

chicken mole

Serves **4**
Preparation time **25 minutes**
Cooking time **45 minutes**

1 tablespoon **sunflower oil**
1 lb **ground chicken**
1 **onion**, roughly chopped
2 **garlic cloves**, finely
  chopped
1 teaspoon **smoked paprika**
½ teaspoon **dried chili seeds**
1 teaspoon **cumin seeds**,
  roughly crushed
13 oz can **chopped tomatoes**
13 oz can **red kidney beans**
⅔ cup **chicken stock**
  (see page 10)
1 tablespoon **dark brown**
  sugar
2 oz **semisweet chocolate**,
  diced
salt and **pepper**

Heat the oil in a saucepan, add the chicken and onion and fry, breaking up the chicken with a wooden spoon until browned. Mix in the garlic, paprika, chili and cumin seeds and cook for 1 minute.

Stir in the tomatoes, beans, stock, and sugar, then mix in the chocolate and seasoning. Cover and simmer gently for 45 minutes, stirring occasionally. Spoon the chili into bowls to serve

For mole toppings, to add to the dish, mix together ½ finely chopped red onion, ½ cored, seeded, diced red bell pepper, 1 halved, pitted, peeled, and diced avocado, the zest and juice of 1 lime, and a small bunch of roughly chopped cilantro. Spoon into a serving bowl. Put 4 oz tortilla chips in a second bowl and 1 cup grated mature cheddar cheese in a third. Allow guests to add their own combination of toppings to the mole.

chicken stacks

Serves **4**
Preparation time **10 minutes**
Cooking time **50–55 minutes**

4 x 4 oz boneless, skinless
  chicken breasts
small bunch **sage**
4 slices **prosciutto**
4 slices **fontina cheese**,
  rind removed
olive oil, for drizzling
salt and **pepper**

Heat a griddle pan (or ordinary skillet). Lay the chicken breasts flat on a board and, using a sharp knife, slice each one horizontally to give 3 flat pieces.

Cook 4 pieces of chicken for 5 minutes on each side. When cooked, arrange these on an oiled baking sheet —these will form the base of the stacks. Put a few sage leaves on top of each one and season.

Cut each length of prosciutto in half and cook 4 pieces for 4 minutes on each side. Place these on top of the chicken. Cut each slice of fontina in half. Top each chicken and prosciutto stack with a piece of cheese.

Griddle or fry the remaining chicken and prosciutto and stack up as before with the cheese and sage, completing each stack with a final layer of chicken. Place the baking sheet in a preheated oven, 350°F, and cook until the cheese is soft, about 5–8 minutes.

Drizzle with a little olive oil, sprinkle with salt and pepper, and garnish with a few sage leaves. Serve with freshly cooked pasta tossed in butter and black pepper.

For tricolore stacks, prepare and fry the chicken as above layering up with 1 extra large sliced tomato and 1 small sliced eggplant, that have both been fried in 1–2 tablespoons olive oil. Instead of adding sage leaves, drizzle each layer with a little pesto. Garnish with basil leaves and Parmesan shavings and serve with a green salad.

sherried chicken strogonoff

Serves **4**

Preparation time **10 minutes**

Cooking time **8–10 minutes**

2 tablespoons **butter**

2 tablespoons **sunflower oil**

4 boneless, skinless **chicken breasts**, cut into long, thin slices

2 **onions**, thinly sliced

1 teaspoon **paprika**

2 teaspoons **mild mustard**

6 tablespoons **dry** or **medium dry sherry**

6 tablespoons **water**

6 tablespoons **sour cream**

salt and **pepper**

Heat the butter and oil in a large skillet, then add the chicken and onions and fry over a medium heat for 6–7 minutes, stirring until the chicken and onions are a deep golden color.

Stir in the paprika, then add the mustard, sherry, water, and seasoning. Cook for 2–3 minutes until the chicken is cooked through, then add the cream and swirl together. Spoon onto plates and serve with rice and green beans.

For chicken & fennel strogonoff, fry the sliced chicken breasts in the butter and oil as above, replacing one of the onions with 1 small, thinly sliced fennel bulb. When golden, add the mustard (but no paprika), 6 tablespoons Pernod instead of the sherry, flaming with a taper, then the water as above. Cook for 2–3 minutes, then add 6 tablespoons crème fraîche or sour cream, stir until just melted, then serve.

chicken kievs

Serves **4**

Preparation time **40 minutes**, plus freezing and chilling

Cooking time **20 minutes**

½ cup **butter**, at room temperature

2 tablespoons chopped **chives**

1 tablespoon chopped **parsley**

2 teaspoons chopped **tarragon** (optional)

1 **garlic clove**, finely chopped

2 teaspoons **lemon juice**

4 boneless, skinless **chicken breasts**, each about 5 oz

2 tablespoons **all-purpose flour**

2 cups **fresh bread crumbs**

2 **eggs**

3 tablespoons **sunflower oil**

pepper

Beat the butter with the herbs, garlic, lemon juice, and a little pepper. Spoon into a line about 10 inches long on a sheet of plastic wrap or foil, then roll up into a neat log shape. Freeze for 15 minutes.

Meanwhile, put one of the chicken breasts between two large sheets of plastic wrap and beat with a rolling pin until it forms a rectangle about ⅛ inch thick, being careful not to make any holes in the chicken. Repeat with the other chicken breasts.

Cut the herb butter into 4 pieces and put one on each chicken breast. Fold in the sides, then the top and bottom, to make a tight parcel.

Put the flour on a plate and the bread crumbs on a second plate, and beat the eggs in a shallow dish. Roll the kievs in the flour, then coat in the egg and roll in the bread crumbs. Put back onto the empty flour plate and chill for 1 hour (longer if you have time).

Heat the oil in a large skillet, add the kievs and cook over a medium heat for 5 minutes, turning until evenly browned. Transfer to a baking sheet, then complete cooking in a preheated oven, 400°F, for 15 minutes or until the chicken is cooked through. Serve with new potatoes and braised red cabbage.

For chicken, garlic, & sundried tomato kievs, chop 2 oz drained sundried tomatoes in oil and stir into ⅔ cup garlic and herb cream cheese. Divide between the flattened chicken breasts, then shape, chill, and cook as above.

moroccan chicken & harissa

Serves **4**
Preparation time **20 minutes**
Cooking time **35 minutes**

1 **onion**, very finely chopped
2 teaspoons **paprika**
1 teaspoon **cumin seeds**
4 x 4 oz boneless, skinless
   chicken breasts
1 bunch **cilantro**, finely
   chopped
4 tablespoons **lemon juice**
3 tablespoons **olive oil**
salt and **pepper**

For the harissa
4 **red bell peppers**
4 large **red chilies**
2 **garlic cloves**, crushed
½ teaspoon **coriander seeds**
1 teaspoon **caraway seeds**
5 tablespoons **olive oil**

Make the harissa by heating a griddle pan (or ordinary skillet). Add the whole bell peppers and cook for 15 minutes, turning occasionally. The skins will blacken and start to lift. Place the peppers in a plastic bag, seal the bag and set aside for a while (this encourages them to "sweat," making it easier to remove their skins). When cool enough to handle, remove the skin, cores, and seeds from the peppers and place the flesh in a blender or food processor.

Remove the skin, cores, and seeds from the red chilies in the same way and add the chili flesh to the blender, together with the garlic, coriander and caraway seeds, and olive oil. Process in the blender to a smooth paste. If not required immediately, place the harissa in a sealable container and pour a thin layer of olive oil over the top. Cover with a lid and refrigerate.

Clean the griddle pan (or ordinary skillet) and reheat it. Place the onion in a bowl, add the paprika and cumin seeds, and mix together. Rub the onion and spice mixture into the chicken breasts. Cook the chicken for 10 minutes on each side, turning once. When cooked, remove from the pan.

Place the cilantro in a bowl and add the lemon juice, olive oil, and a little seasoning. Add the chicken to the bowl and toss well. Serve with rice and the harissa.

For a spinach salad, as an accompaniment, rinse and tear 8 cups spinach and add to a pan with any residual water. Cover and cook for 1–2 minutes until wilted. Stir in 1 chopped garlic clove, 6 tablespoons Greek or whole milk yogurt, salt, and pepper. Warm and serve.

chicken & mushroom lasagna

Serves **4–6**
Preparation time **45 minutes**
Cooking time **1 hour
25 minutes**

8 **chicken thighs**
⅔ cup **dry white wine**
1¼ cups **chicken stock**
(see page 10)
few stems **thyme**
2 tablespoons **olive oil**
2 **onions**, thinly sliced
2 **garlic cloves**, finely chopped
4 oz **exotic mushrooms**
4 oz **shiitake mushrooms**,
sliced
¼ cup **butter**
½ cup **all-purpose flour**
¾ cup **heavy cream**
8 oz pack of 6 **fresh lasagna
sheets**
6 tablespoons freshly grated
Parmesan cheese
salt and **pepper**

Pack the chicken thighs into the base of a saucepan,
add the wine, stock, thyme, and a little seasoning.
Bring to a boil, then cover and simmer for 45 minutes
until tender.

Meanwhile, heat the oil in a skillet, add the onions
and fry for 5 minutes until just turning golden. Mix in
the garlic and cook for 2–3 minutes, then stir in the
mushrooms and fry for 2–3 minutes until golden.

Lift the chicken out of the pan, drain, and set aside.
Pour the stock into a measuring cup. Make up to
2½ cups with water if needed. Wash and dry the pan,
then melt the butter in it. Stir in the flour, then gradually
beat in the stock and bring to a boil, stirring until
thickened and smooth. Stir in the cream and adjust
the seasoning, if needed.

Soak the lasagna sheets in boiling water for 5 minutes.
Cut the skin and bones away from the chicken and
dice the meat. Drain the lasagna sheets.

Pour a thin layer of sauce into the base of an
8 x 11 x 2 inch ovenproof dish or roasting pan, then
cover with 2 sheets of the lasagna. Spoon over half the
mushroom mixture and half the chicken, then cover with
a thin layer of sauce. Repeat the layers, then cover with
the remaining lasagna and sauce. Sprinkle with the
Parmesan and set aside until required.

Cook in a preheated oven, 375°F, for 40 minutes until
piping hot and the top is golden. Serve with salad and
garlic bread.

griddled tandoori chicken

Serves **4**

Preparation time **10 minutes**, plus marinating

Cooking time **16–20 minutes**

4 x 4 oz boneless, skinless **chicken breasts**

4 tablespoons **tandoori paste** or **powder**

2 **red onions**, finely sliced

4 **tomatoes**, finely sliced

1 bunch **cilantro**, roughly chopped

4 tablespoons **lemon juice**

4 tablespoons **olive oil**

lemon wedges, griddled (optional), to serve

salt and **pepper**

Using a sharp knife, make a series of small slashes in the flesh of the chicken breasts and rub in the tandoori paste or powder. Allow to marinate in the refrigerator overnight.

Heat a griddle pan (or ordinary skillet). Cook the marinated chicken breasts for 8–10 minutes on each side, allowing the authentic tandoori charred color to appear, or until cooked thoroughly.

Mix the red onions, tomatoes, and cilantro together with the lemon juice, olive oil, and seasoning in a small bowl. Serve the salad with the tandoori chicken, accompanied by lemon wedges, griddled if desired.

For griddled harissa chicken, rub the slashed chicken with 4 teaspoons harissa paste instead of the tandoori paste or powder. Marinate then fry. Soak 1 cup couscous in 1¾ cups boiling water for 5 minutes. Stir in 2 tablespoons olive oil, 3 tablespoons fresh chopped cilantro, and seasoning. Serve with lemon wedges.

cidered chicken puff pie

Serves **4**
Preparation time **40 minutes**
Cooking time **1 hour
20 minutes**

8 **chicken thighs**
1¼ cups **dry hard cider**
1¼ cups **chicken stock**
(see page 10)
2 small **leeks**, slit, rinsed,
sliced
¼ cup **butter**
½ cup **all-purpose flour**
1 tablespoon chopped
tarragon
2 tablespoons chopped
parsley
1 lb **puff pastry**
flour, for dusting
1 **egg**, beaten, to glaze
salt and **pepper**

Pack the chicken thighs into a saucepan, pour over the cider and stock, then season. Cover and simmer for 45 minutes.

Lift the chicken onto a plate, and simmer the leeks in the stock for 4–5 minutes. Strain the leeks, reserving the stock in a measuring cup. Make up the stock to 2½ cups with water, if needed.

Wash and dry the pan, then melt the butter in it. Stir in the flour, then gradually beat in the stock and bring to a boil, stirring until thickened. Mix in the herbs and season.

Dice the chicken, discarding the skin and bones. Put into a 5 cup pie dish with the leeks. Pour over the sauce.

Roll out the pastry on a floured surface until a little larger than the top of the pie dish. Cut 4 strips about ½ inch wide and stick along the rim with a little egg. Brush the top of the strip with egg, then press the pastry lid in place. Trim off the excess and crimp the edge. Cut leaves from the excess and add.

Glaze the pastry lid and bake in a preheated oven, 400°F, for 30 minutes until golden.

For chicken, frankfurter, & corn puff pie, cook 6 chicken thighs as above, and add the meat to the pie dish with 4 thickly sliced, chilled frankfurters. Replace the leeks with a 7 oz drained can of corn. Omit the herbs from the sauce and flavor with 1 teaspoon English mustard, then continue as above.

thai red chicken curry

Serves **4**
Preparation time **15 minutes**
Cooking time **35 minutes**

3 **shallots**, finely chopped
3 **garlic cloves**, finely
  chopped
1 tablespoon **sunflower oil**
2 tablespoons **red Thai curry
  paste**
2 teaspoons **galangal paste**
  (from a jar)
1⅔ cups **low-fat coconut milk**
2 teaspoons **fish sauce**
1 teaspoon **light brown sugar**
3 dried **kaffir lime leaves**
6 **chicken thighs**, skinned,
  boned, diced
Thai basil leaves, optional

Fry the shallots and garlic in the oil in a medium saucepan for 3–4 minutes until softened. Stir in the curry paste and galangal and cook for 1 minute. Mix in the coconut milk, fish sauce, sugar, and lime leaves and bring to a boil.

Stir in the chicken, then cover and simmer for 30 minutes, stirring occasionally until the chicken is cooked through. Stir in the basil leaves, if desired, and serve in bowls with boiled rice.

For Thai green chicken curry, make the curry as above, adding 2 peeled and finely chopped lemon grass stems when frying the shallots and garlic. Stir in 2 tablespoons green Thai curry paste, then the remaining ingredients as above. Finish by stirring in the grated zest of 1 lime and lime juice to taste. Garnish with fresh cilantro.

baked chicken in a salt crust

Serves **4**
Preparation time **20 minutes**
Cooking time **2 hours**

10 cups **salt**
3 lb **whole chicken**
1 **garlic bulb**
3–4 stems **rosemary**
⅔ cup **water**

For the red pepper ketchup
4 whole **red peppers** from a
  jar of roasted sweet peppers
  in water, drained
1 tablespoon **sweet Thai chili
  dipping sauce**
1 tablespoon **olive oil**
1 tablespoon **balsamic
  vinegar**
black pepper, to taste

Line an ovenproof casserole dish or roasting pan (large enough to hold the salt and chicken) with two large pieces of foil. Pour a thin layer of salt into the base, then sit the chicken on top. Cut the garlic in half through the center, then put both halves into the body cavity of the chicken with one of the rosemary stems. Tear the leaves from the other stems and sprinkle over the chicken.

Pour the remaining salt over the chicken, pulling up the foil to contain the salt in an even thickness around the chicken. Drizzle the measured water over the top, then spread the dampened salt into an even layer over the breast. Seal the edges of the foil tightly.

Bake in a preheated oven, 375°F, for 2 hours. Loosen the edge of the foil, then lift the package out. Open the foil and crack the salt crust away from the chicken.

To make the ketchup, remove one of the cooked half garlic bulbs from inside the chicken cavity, discarding the papery skins, and put into a food processor with the other ketchup ingredients. Puree until smooth. Brush the salt off the chicken with a pastry brush, then carve normally and serve with the ketchup, salad, and warm ciabatta bread.

For baked chicken with aïoli, cook the chicken as above, then take all the garlic cloves out of their skins and pound to a paste in a mortar and pestle with a pinch of the baking salt. Mix with ⅔ cup good-quality bought mayonnaise and season with coarsely crushed black pepper.

chicken with chili and ginger jam

Serves **4**
Preparation time **5 minutes**
Cooking time **25 minutes**

4 x 4 oz boneless **chicken
breasts**
rice noodles, to serve
cilantro leaves, to garnish

For the chili and ginger jam
3 **chilies**, cored, seeded,
chopped
1 **garlic clove**, crushed
1 **onion**, chopped
2 inch piece **ginger root**,
peeled, chopped
½ cup **white vinegar**
2 cups **sugar**

To make the chili and ginger jam, place the chopped
chilies, garlic, chopped onion, and ginger in a small
saucepan. Add the white vinegar and sugar. Bring to
a boil, then reduce the heat and allow to simmer for
15 minutes. The mixture should be thick, sticky, and
jam-like, and will become more so as it cools.

Meanwhile, heat a griddle pan (or ordinary skillet).
Cook the chicken breasts, skin side down, for
8–10 minutes. Turn the chicken over and cook for an
additional 8–10 minutes, or until cooked thoroughly.

Serve the chicken on a bed of noodles, with the chili
and ginger jam poured over the top, and garnish with
cilantro leaves. Store any remaining chili jam in the
refrigerator, covered, for up to 1 week.

For chicken salad with chili dressing, cook the
chicken as above. Mix ½ diced cucumber in a salad
bowl with ½ thinly sliced red onion, 15 halved cherry
tomatoes, 2 small crisphead lettuces, torn into leaves,
and a small bunch of mint, torn into pieces. Fork the
juice of 2 limes, 1 tablespoon Thai chili dipping sauce,
1 tablespoon soy sauce, 1 teaspoon dark brown
sugar together. Add the chicken to the salad and
drizzle with dressing.

chicken and barley risotto

Serves **4**
Preparation time **15 minutes**
Cooking time **1 hour
10 minutes**

2 tablespoons **olive oil**
6 boneless, skinless **chicken thighs**, diced
1 **onion**, roughly chopped
2 **garlic cloves**, finely chopped
7 oz **chestnut mushrooms**, sliced
1¼ cups **pearl barley**
¾ cup **red wine**
5 cups **chicken stock**
(see page 10)
salt and **pepper**

To garnish
parsley, chopped
shavings of **Parmesan cheese**

Heat the oil in a large skillet, add the chicken and onion and fry for 5 minutes, stirring until lightly browned.

Stir in the garlic and mushrooms and fry for 2 minutes, then mix in the barley. Add the red wine, half the stock, and plenty of seasoning, then bring to a boil, stirring. Cover and simmer for 1 hour, topping up with extra stock as needed until the barley is soft.

Spoon into shallow bowls and garnish with the parsley and Parmesan. Serve with garlic bread and salad.

For chicken & red rice risotto, fry the chicken and 1 chopped red onion as above. Add the garlic and ½ cup skinned and diced tomatoes in place of the mushrooms. Stir in 1¼ cups red Camargue rice, cook for 1 minute, then add the wine. Gradually add 5 cups of hot chicken stock, ladle by ladle as needed, only adding more once the rice has absorbed the previous ladleful. Cook for 25 minutes until the chicken and rice are tender. Top with 4 oz crumbled St Agur or Roquefort cheese.

southern fried chicken

Serves **4**

Preparation time **25 minutes**

Cooking time **35–40 minutes**

1 lb **sweet potatoes**, peeled

1 lb **baking potatoes**,
   scrubbed

6 tablespoons **sunflower oil**

1½ teaspoons **smoked
   paprika**

1½ teaspoons **dried oregano**

1 teaspoon **powdered
   mustard**

1 teaspoon **dried red pepper
   flakes**

4 tablespoons **all-purpose
   flour**

2 **eggs**

2 tablespoons **water**

2¼ cups **fresh bread crumbs**

4 **chicken thigh** and
   drumstick joints

salt and **pepper**

Thickly slice the sweet and baking potatoes, then cut
into thick wedges. Mix 3 tablespoons of the oil with
1 teaspoon paprika, 1 teaspoon oregano, ½ teaspoon
mustard, ½ teaspoon pepper flakes, and some salt in a
large plastic bag or bowl. Add the potatoes and toss
in the oil mixture.

Mix the remaining paprika, oregano, mustard, pepper
flakes, and seasoning with the flour on a large plate.
Beat the eggs and measured water in a shallow dish
and put the bread crumbs on a second large plate.

Coat the chicken pieces in the flour mixture, then
the beaten egg, then the bread crumbs, until
completely covered.

Heat a large roasting pan in the oven, 400°F, for
5 minutes. Meanwhile, heat the remaining oil in a
large skillet, add the chicken and fry until pale golden.
Transfer the chicken to the hot roasting pan, add the
potatoes and roast for 30–35 minutes until the chicken
is cooked through and the potatoes crisp and golden.
Transfer to serving plates and serve with mayonnaise
and salad.

For cheesy fried chicken escalopes, make up the
vegetables as above, then mix the remaining paprika,
pepper flakes, and a little salt and pepper with the
flour. Coat 4 skinless, boneless chicken breasts,
each cut into thin flat slices, in the flour mixture,
then in the beaten egg, then in 2 cups fresh bread
crumbs mixed with 2 tablespoons grated Parmesan
cheese. Fry in the oil for 10–12 minutes until golden
and cooked through.

chicken qdra

Serves **4**

Preparation time **15 minutes**

Cooking time **2 hours
5 minutes**

2 tablespoons **olive oil**

8 boneless, skinless **chicken
thighs**, cut into large chunks

2 **onions**, thinly sliced

2 **garlic cloves**, finely
chopped

2 tablespoons **all-purpose
flour**

3¾ cups **chicken stock**
(see page 10)

grated zest and juice of
1 lemon

2 large pinches **saffron
threads**

1 **cinnamon stick**, halved

2 x 13½ oz cans **chickpeas**,
drained

1 lb **potatoes**, cut into chunks

parsley or **mixed parsley and
mint**, chopped, to garnish

salt and **pepper**

Heat the oil in a large skillet, add the chicken and onions, frying in batches if needed for 5 minutes until golden.

Stir in the garlic, then mix in the flour. Add the stock, lemon zest and juice, saffron, cinnamon, and plenty of seasoning and bring to a boil. Transfer to a tagine or casserole dish. Add the chickpeas and potatoes, mix together, then cover. Cook in a preheated oven, 350°F, for 2 hours.

Stir, then sprinkle with the herbs. Spoon into shallow bowls and serve with warm pita breads.

For saffron chicken with mixed vegetables, reduce the stock to 2½ cups and add a 13 oz can of chopped tomatoes. Add 1 can of chickpeas only, then mix in ¾ cup thickly sliced okra and 4 oz thickly sliced green beans 10 minutes before the end of cooking.

chinese lemon chicken

Serves **4**
Preparation time **25 minutes**,
  plus marinating
Cooking time **12 minutes**

4 tablespoons **cornstarch**
1 tablespoon **dry sherry**
1 **egg**
grated zest of **1 lemon**
2 large boneless, skinless
  chicken breasts, cut into
  thin crosswise slices
6 tablespoons **sunflower oil**

For the lemon sauce
2 tablespoons **cornstarch**
juice of **1 lemon**
2 tablespoons **dry sherry**
4 teaspoons **superfine sugar**
1¼ cups **chicken stock**
  (see page 10)
3 **scallions**, thinly sliced
salt and **pepper**

Mix the cornstarch with the sherry and egg until smooth, then stir in the lemon zest and a little seasoning. Add the chicken slices and toss together, then allow to marinate for 30 minutes.

Make the sauce by mixing the cornstarch in a saucepan with a little of the lemon juice until smooth. Stir in the remaining lemon juice, sherry, sugar, and seasoning. Put the pan on the heat and gradually beat in the stock. Bring to a boil, beating until clear, thickened, and smooth. Take off the heat and add the scallions.

Add the oil to a wok or large skillet, heat, then add the chicken a few pieces at a time and cook for 4–5 minutes, turning until golden and cooked through. Lift the chicken out of the pan with a draining spoon, put it on a plate lined with paper towels and keep it hot. Cook the remaining chicken in the same way.

Reheat the sauce. Transfer the chicken to small bowls lined with rice, spoon a little of the sauce over the top, pour the remaining sauce into a separate bowl, then hand round so that guests can add sauce to taste.

For salt & pepper chicken, omit the lemon zest from the egg and cornstarch batter, adding a large pinch of salt and ½ teaspoon roughly crushed Szechuan peppercorns. Fry in oil as above and serve with sweet Thai chili dipping sauce.

italian chicken cushion

Serves **4**

Preparation time **30 minutes**

Cooking time **1 hour 30 minutes**

3 lb **whole chicken**, boned

13 oz **Sicilian sausages** or **other gourmet flavored sausages** (such as Parmesan and pancetta)

4 **scallions**, finely chopped

1 large **whole red pepper**, from a jar of roasted sweet peppers in water, drained, diced

3 oz **sundried tomatoes** in oil, drained, roughly chopped

⅓ cup pitted **olives**, roughly chopped

3 tablespoons chopped **basil**

1 cup **fresh bread crumbs**

1 **egg yolk**

1 tablespoon **olive oil** or **oil from the sundried tomato jar**

salt and **pepper**

Put the boned chicken on a large cutting board with the breast skin downward, neaten up the edges with a knife and open out flat.

Slit the sausages lengthwise, peel off the skins and put the meat into a large bowl. Add the scallions, red pepper, sundried tomatoes, olives, basil, bread crumbs, egg yolk, and plenty of seasoning and mix with a wooden spoon. Spoon onto the center of the chicken. Fold the legs, wings, and remaining skin back into position so that the stuffing is enclosed. Tie with string like the spokes of a wheel, adjusting the string and patting into shape to form a round cushion.

Weigh the joint, then put it breast side up in a roasting pan. Drizzle with the oil and season lightly. Cover with foil and roast in a preheated oven, 375°F, for 20 minutes per 1 lb plus 20 minutes. Remove the foil for the last 30 minutes and baste the chicken once or twice with pan juices until a deep golden brown and cooked when tested (see page 11).

Allow to cool, remove the string, and cut into wedge shapes. Serve with salad.

For chicken cushion with ginger & cranberries, use plain good-quality sausages rather than highly flavored ones, remove the skins and mix with the chopped scallions, red pepper, bread crumbs, and egg yolk as above, then flavor with a 1½ inch piece of grated ginger root, the grated zest of 1 small orange, 3 tablespoons chopped parsley, and ½ cup dried cranberries. Serve hot with roast potatoes.

chicken bisteeya

Serves **6**

Preparation time **40 minutes**

Cooking time **1 hour 50 minutes**

4 **chicken thigh** and **drumstick joints**

1 **onion**, chopped

1 **cinnamon stick**, halved

1 inch piece **ginger root**, finely chopped

¼ teaspoon **turmeric**

2½ cups **water**

3 tablespoons chopped **cilantro**

3 tablespoons chopped **parsley**

¼ cup **raisins**

⅓ cup **blanched almonds**, roughly chopped

4 **eggs**

7 oz pack chilled **phyllo pastry**

5 tablespoons **butter**, melted

salt and **pepper**

To garnish

confectioners' sugar, sifted

ground cinnamon

Pack the chicken into a large saucepan and sprinkle the onion over the top, then add the cinnamon, ginger, turmeric, and seasoning. Cover the chicken with the measured water. Cover and simmer for 1 hour until tender. Lift the chicken out of the stock and put on a plate to cool. Boil the stock rapidly for about 10 minutes until reduced to one-third.

Dice the chicken, discarding the skin and bones. Strain the stock into a pitcher. Discard the cinnamon stick, then add the herbs, raisins, and almonds to the chicken. Beat ¾ cup stock with the eggs.

Brush a 9 inch springform pan with a little of the melted butter. Unroll the pastry, then place one of the sheets in the pan so that it half covers the base and drapes up over the side and hangs over the top of the pan. Add a second pastry sheet overlapping a little over the first and brush with a little melted butter. Continue adding pastry, brushing alternate sheets with melted butter until two-thirds of the pastry has been used and the pan is thickly covered.

Spoon in the chicken mixture, then cover with the eggs and stock. Arrange the remaining pastry over the top in a smooth layer, then fold in the sides in soft pleats, brushing layers of pastry with butter as you go. Brush the top layer with the remaining butter, then bake in a preheated oven, 350°F, for 40–45 minutes until golden brown and the filling is set.

Allow to cool for 15 minutes, remove from the pan, and transfer to a cutting board. Dust lightly with confectioners' sugar and cinnamon and serve warm.

chicken risotto

Serves **6**
Preparation time **35 minutes**
Cooking time **2 hours**

2 lb **whole chicken**
8 cups **water**
2 **celery sticks**
2 **onions**
2 **carrots**
3–4 tablespoons **olive oil**
7 tablespoons **white wine**
12 oz **tomatoes**, skinned and
  mashed
2½ cups **risotto rice**
⅛ cup **butter**, softened
¾ cup freshly grated
  Parmesan cheese
1–2 tablespoons chopped
  parsley, to garnish
salt and **pepper**

Remove the bones from the chicken and place them in a large pan with the water. Add 1 celery stick, 1 onion, 1 carrot, and seasoning. Cover and simmer for 1½ hours. Strain the stock and keep hot.

Meanwhile, dice the chicken meat, discarding all the skin. Finely chop the remaining celery, onion, and carrot. Heat the oil, add the chopped vegetables and sauté until lightly browned. Add the chicken and cook, stirring for 5 minutes. Add the wine and cook, stirring, until it has evaporated.

Add the tomatoes and season to taste. Cover and cook over a low heat for 20 minutes, adding a little of the hot chicken stock if the mixture becomes dry.

Add the rice, then add the hot stock, a large ladleful at a time, stirring until each addition is absorbed into the rice. Continue adding stock in this way, cooking for 20 minutes until the rice is creamy.

Remove from the heat, add the butter and Parmesan and fold in gently. Cover and allow the risotto to rest for a few minutes before serving, sprinkled with parsley.

For chicken risotto with wild mushrooms, make the stock as above then fry just the celery and onion in oil for the base of the risotto. Add the diced chicken and continue adding stock until the risotto is almost cooked. In a separate skillet, melt half the butter then add 4 oz exotic mushrooms, 4 oz sliced shiitake mushrooms, and 2 finely chopped garlic cloves, stirring until golden. Stir the remaining butter and Parmesan into the risotto, spoon into bowls, and top with the mushrooms.

stilton-stuffed chicken with ham

Serves **4**
Preparation time **25 minutes**
Cooking time **30 minutes**

4 boneless, skinless **chicken breasts**, each about 5 oz
4 oz **Stilton cheese**, rind removed
2 oz **sundried tomatoes** in oil, drained
4 slices **prosciutto**
salt and **pepper**

Cut a slit through the side of each chicken breast, then enlarge to make a small pocket. Cut the cheese into 4 slices, then tuck one slice into each chicken pocket with 1–2 pieces of tomato depending on their size. Sprinkle the outside of the chicken breasts with seasoning.

Wrap each chicken breast with a slice of prosciutto and put in a roasting pan.

Bake in a preheated oven, 400°F, for 30 minutes until the chicken is cooked when tested (see page 11). Thickly slice the chicken or leave whole if preferred. Transfer to serving plates and serve with purple sprouting broccoli and buttery new potatoes.

For chicken cordon bleu, slit the chicken as above, then fill with 4 oz Gruyère cheese with its rind removed and cut into 4 slices, and 2 halved slices of smoked ham. Secure the pockets closed with toothpicks, then fry in 2 tablespoons butter and 1 tablespoon olive oil for 15 minutes, turning the chicken until golden and cooked through. Deglaze the pan with ⅔ cup white wine or stock and cook for 3–4 minutes until the chicken is cooked through. Stir in 4 tablespoons heavy cream, then remove the toothpicks and serve.

chicken with pimento puree

Serves **8**

Preparation time **15 minutes**, plus cooling

Cooking time **1 hour 45 minutes–2 hours 15 minutes**

4 lb **whole chicken**

1 **onion**, quartered

1 **carrot**, sliced

2 **celery sticks**, sliced

4 **juniper berries**, crushed

1 **bay leaf**

4–6 stalks **parsley**

6 **peppercorns**, lightly crushed

zucchini slices, griddled, to serve (optional)

parsley, chopped, to garnish

salt

For the pimento puree

8 oz canned **pimentos**, drained, rinsed, chopped

1 tablespoon **tomato paste**

2 tablespoons **mango chutney**

¾ cup **low-fat plain yogurt**

salt and **pepper**

Put the chicken, onion, carrot, celery, juniper berries, bay leaf, parsley, peppercorns, and salt into a saucepan. Cover with water. Bring to a boil, cover the saucepan, and simmer for 1½–2 hours, or until the chicken is cooked when tested (see page 11). Allow the chicken to cool in the stock. Lift out the chicken, drain and dry it. Reserve the stock, discarding the bay leaf. Skin the chicken and slice the meat from the bones.

To make the puree, put the pimentos, 2 tablespoons of the reserved chicken stock, tomato paste, and chutney into a saucepan and bring to a boil. Transfer to a blender or food processor and blend until smooth. Set aside to cool. Blend the cooled pimento mixture with the yogurt and season to taste.

Arrange the chicken on a serving dish and pour over the sauce. Garnish with the parsley and serve with griddled zucchini, if desired.

For mini chicken meatballs with pimento puree, mix 1 lb ground chicken with 3 chopped scallions, 2 finely chopped garlic cloves, 1 egg yolk, and seasoning. Shape into 20 small meatballs, chill for 30 minutes then fry in 1 tablespoon sunflower oil for 5 minutes. Transfer to a preheated oven, 375°F, for 15 minutes until cooked through. Serve with the sauce as above, rice, and a tomato and onion salad.

lemon grass chicken & vegetables

Serves **4**

Preparation time **15 minutes**,
  plus soaking

Cooking time **about
  10 minutes**

18 stalks **lemon grass**

8 boneless, skinless **chicken
  thighs**

1 **garlic clove**

2 **kaffir lime leaves**

2 tablespoons **soy sauce**

1 tablespoon **sesame oil**

1 **red bell pepper**, cored,
  seeded, sliced

1 **green bell pepper**, cored,
  seeded, sliced

12 oz **sugar snap peas**

2 **bok choy**, quartered
  lengthwise

Place 16 of the lemon grass stalks in a bowl of water and allow to soak for 1 hour. Chop the remaining 2 stalks.

Put the chicken, chopped lemon grass, garlic, lime leaves, and half the soy sauce in a food processor and process until well combined. Divide the mixture into 16 portions and mold each portion around a piece of the soaked lemon grass.

Place on a baking sheet, drizzle with half the oil, and cook under a hot broiler for 4–5 minutes, turning occasionally, until golden and cooked through.

Heat the remaining oil in a wok or skillet, add the vegetables and stir-fry for 2–3 minutes until just tender, then add the remaining soy sauce. Serve the stir-fried vegetables with the chicken.

For stir-fried lemon grass chicken, thinly slice 3 boneless skinless chicken breasts. Finely chop 2 lemon grass stalks, the garlic and lime leaves. Heat 2 teaspoons sesame oil and 2 teaspoons sunflower oil in a wok, add the chicken and stir-fry for 6–7 minutes. Add the chopped lemon grass, garlic, and lime leaves then the vegetables and stir-fry for 2–3 minutes until the vegetables are just tender and the chicken is cooked through. Mix in 2 tablespoons soy sauce, 2 tablespoons dry sherry, and 4 tablespoons water or stock, bring to a boil then serve with egg fried rice.

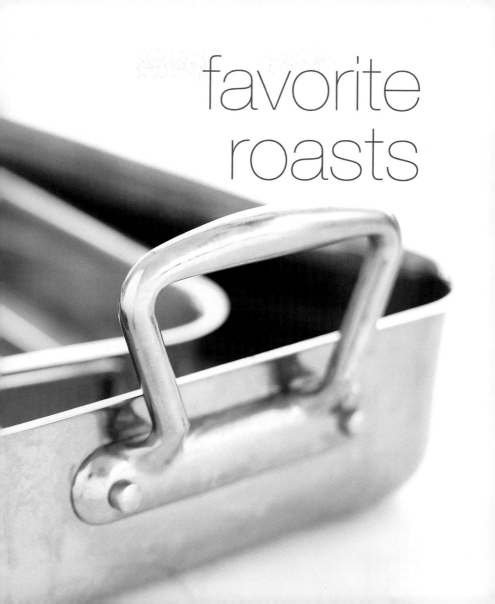

favorite
roasts

pot-roast chicken with vermouth

Serves **4**
Preparation time **20 minutes**
Cooking time **1 hour**
  40 minutes–1 hour
  50 minutes

1 tablespoon **olive oil**
7 oz **shallots**, peeled, halved
2 slices **Canadian bacon**,
  diced
2 **garlic cloves**, finely
  chopped
1 lb **baby new potatoes**
2 tablespoons **butter**
3 lb **whole chicken**
4 **celery sticks**, each cut into
  3 sections
8 oz **baby carrots**, large ones
  halved
3 **bay leaves**
¾ cup **dry vermouth**
¾ cup **chicken stock**
  (see page 10)
2 tablespoons chopped
  parsley, to garnish (optional)
salt and **pepper**

Heat the oil in a large flameproof casserole, add the shallots and bacon and fry for 3–4 minutes over a medium heat until just beginning to brown. Add the garlic and potatoes and fry until just beginning to brown. Tip onto a plate.

Add the butter to the pan and, when melted, add the chicken, breast side downward. Fry on each breast until golden, then turn over and fry the underside. Return the fried vegetables to the pan and tuck the celery and carrots around the sides of the chicken, adding the bay leaves and a little salt and pepper.

Pour in the vermouth and stock, then bring to a boil. Cover with a tight-fitting lid and transfer to a preheated oven, 375°F, for 1¼ hours. Spoon the vermouth juices over the chicken, then cook uncovered for 20–30 minutes until golden and cooked when tested (see page 11).

Lift the chicken onto a serving plate, scoop the vegetables out with a draining spoon and nestle them around the chicken. Cover with foil and keep hot. Boil the remaining pan juices for about 5 minutes or until reduced by half, then pour into a pitcher and sprinkle the vegetables with the parsley, if desired. Carve as for a traditional roast and serve with the gravy.

For pot-roast chicken with cider & mustard, omit the garlic and vermouth, adding ¾ cup dry hard cider and 2 teaspoons Dijon mustard. Continue as above.

roast chicken with lemon baste

Serves **4–5**
Preparation time **35 minutes**
Cooking time **1 hour
30 minutes**

3½ lb **whole chicken**
½ cup **full-fat cream cheese**
3 tablespoons **olive oil**
1 oz **preserved lemon**, well
  drained, seeded, finely
  chopped
½ cup finely chopped mixed
  fresh **basil** and **parsley**
3 **garlic cloves**, finely
  chopped
1 lb 6 oz small **new potatoes**,
  scrubbed
8 oz **chantenay carrots**,
  scrubbed
4 oz **baby corn**
7 oz **fine asparagus**, trimmed
¾ cup **dry white wine**
¾ cup **chicken stock**
  (see page 10)
salt and **cayenne pepper**

Remove the trussing elastic from the chicken and set aside. Insert a small sharp knife between the skin and the flesh at the top of one of the breasts, then enlarge to make a small slit. Slide a finger into the slit and gently move the finger to lift the skin away from the chicken breast and make a pocket, being careful not to tear the skin. Do the same from the base of the breast until the skin is completely loosened, then continue over the top of the leg. Repeat on the other chicken breast and leg.

Mix the cream cheese with 1 tablespoon of the oil, and add the lemon, herbs, garlic, salt, and cayenne pepper. Lift small amounts of the cheese mix at a time onto a round-bladed knife and insert into the pocket beneath the chicken skin until it has all been added. Ease it into an even layer by pressing the outside of the skin.

Transfer the chicken to a roasting pan and reshape it by twisting the trussing elastic around the legs and parson's nose. Cover with oiled foil and roast in a preheated oven, 375°F, for 50 minutes. Baste the chicken with the pan juices, then re-cover. Add the potatoes, carrots, and remaining oil (but do not cover these with foil) and roast for 30 minutes, turning once. Remove the foil from the chicken, baste, and add the corn and asparagus. Roast for 10 minutes until the asparagus is just tender and the chicken cooked when tested (see page 11).

Transfer to a serving plate, add the wine and stock to the roasting pan and bring to a boil on the stovetop, scraping up the residue in the pan and seasoning to taste. Strain into a pitcher and serve with the chicken.

roast chicken with spice rub

Serves **4**

Preparation time **20 minutes**

Cooking time **1 hour
20 minutes–1 hour
30 minutes**

3 lb **whole chicken**

3 tablespoons **olive oil**

1 teaspoon **fennel seeds**,
roughly crushed

1 teaspoon **cumin seeds**,
roughly crushed

1 teaspoon **dried red pepper
flakes**

1 teaspoon **dried oregano**

½ teaspoon **ground cinnamon**

1¼ lb **baby new potatoes**

2 **shallots**, finely chopped

2 **garlic cloves**, finely
chopped (optional)

5 oz **fine green beans**

juice of **1 lemon**

¾ cup **chicken stock**
(see page 10)

small bunch **cilantro** or **flat-
leaf parsley**, or mix of the
two, roughly chopped

salt and **pepper**

Put the chicken into a large roasting pan and drizzle with 2 tablespoons of the oil. Mix the crushed seeds, pepper flakes, oregano, and cinnamon with some salt and pepper, then sprinkle half over the chicken.

Cover the chicken loosely with foil, then roast in a preheated oven, 375°F, for 40 minutes. Remove the foil and baste with the pan juices. Add the potatoes to the pan, toss in the juices, then cook uncovered for 40–50 minutes, basting and turning the potatoes once or twice until golden brown. Re-cover the chicken with foil if the spice rub begins to overbrown.

Meanwhile, heat the remaining oil in a small saucepan, add the shallots and garlic, if desired, and fry for 5 minutes until softened. Stir in the remaining spice rub and cook for 1 minute. Cook the green beans in a saucepan of boiling water for 5 minutes, then drain and toss in the shallot mixture with the lemon juice.

When the chicken is cooked (see page 11), add the green-bean mixture to the potatoes. Mix together, then add the stock and bring to a boil on the stovetop. Sprinkle with the herbs, carve the chicken, and serve.

For roast chicken with herbes de Provence, roughly chop the leaves from 3 stems of rosemary, 3 stems of thyme and 2 lavender flowers. Mix with 1 teaspoon coarse salt and ¼ teaspoon roughly crushed colored peppercorns. Sprinkle half over the chicken and the rest over the potatoes. Continue as above.

roast chicken with spiced roots

Serves **4**
Preparation time **30 minutes**
Cooking time **1 hour
20 minutes**

3 lb **whole chicken**
2 teaspoons **coriander seeds**
1 teaspoon **fennel seeds**
1 teaspoon **cumin seeds**
2 tablespoons **olive oil**
½ teaspoon **turmeric**
½ teaspoon **paprika**
2 **parsnips**
2 large **carrots**
2 **sweet potatoes**
1 large **onion**
8 **garlic cloves**, unpeeled
cilantro leaves, to garnish

For the gravy
2 tablespoons **all-purpose
flour**
1¾ cups **chicken stock**
(see page 10)

Place the chicken in a large roasting pan. Crush the seeds and put them in a large plastic bag with the oil, turmeric, and paprika. Shake until well mixed. Spoon a little of the mixture over the chicken breast, then cover with foil.

Roast the chicken in a preheated oven, 375°F, for 1 hour 20 minutes.

Cut the vegetables into large chunks, add to the bag of spiced oil and toss. Add to the roasting pan after 20 minutes of cooking the chicken, tucking some garlic cloves between the chicken legs and adding the rest to the vegetables. Cook for 1 hour until golden, turning the vegetables after 30 minutes and removing the foil from the chicken at this point.

Transfer the chicken and vegetables from the roasting pan to a large serving plate and keep warm. Garnish with cilantro.

Drain the fat from the meat juices and stir in the flour. To make the gravy, put the roasting pan on the stovetop and cook for 1 minute, stirring. Gradually stir in the stock and bring to a boil. Strain into a pitcher and serve with the carved chicken and vegetables.

For barbecued spiced chicken, mix the spices and oil in a plastic bag as above then add 8 boneless, skinless chicken thighs that have been slashed once or twice with a small knife. Toss together then cook over a medium hot barbecue for about 20 minutes, turning once or twice until browned and cooked through. Serve with cucumber raita and shredded lettuce.

roast chicken with sage & onion

Serves **4**
Preparation time **30 minutes**
Cooking time **1 hour
30 minutes–1 hour
40 minutes**

12 slices **bacon**
16 **pork cocktail sausages**
1 **onion**, chopped
1 tablespoon **sunflower oil**
small bunch **sage**, plus extra
to garnish
3 cups **fresh bread crumbs**
grated zest of 1 **lemon**
1 **egg**, beaten
3 lb **whole chicken**
2 tablespoons **butter**
salt and **pepper**

For the gravy
2 tablespoons **all-purpose
flour**
1¾ cups **chicken stock**
(see page 10)
salt and **pepper**

Halve 8 bacon slices, then wrap a half around each sausage and set aside.

Fry the onion in the oil for 5 minutes until softened. Finely chop some of the sage to give about 2 tablespoons. Mix this with the onions, bread crumbs, lemon zest, egg, and a little seasoning. Shape two-thirds of the sage stuffing into 8 small balls, then spoon the remainder into the body cavity of the chicken. Put the chicken in a roasting pan, cover the breast with the remaining sage leaves, season, and dot with butter, then arrange the remaining bacon on top.

Cover the chicken loosely with foil, then roast in a preheated oven, 375°F, for 1 hour. Remove the foil, baste the chicken, and add the stuffing balls and wrapped sausages to the bottom of the pan. Roast uncovered for 30–40 minutes until golden and cooked when tested (see page 11).

Transfer the chicken, stuffing balls, and sausages to a serving plate and keep hot. Pour the fat out of the roasting pan to leave just the meat juices. Put the pan on the stovetop and stir in the flour. Cook for 1 minute, then gradually mix in the stock, bring to a boil, stirring until thickened. Season and strain into a pitcher. Serve with roast potatoes and vegetables, garnished with sage.

For roast chicken with apricot & walnut stuffing, omit the sage and lemon zest from the stuffing, adding the grated zest of ½ orange, ⅓ cup ready-to-eat dried apricots, chopped, and ¼ cup roughly chopped walnuts. Tuck 2 bay leaves under the bacon on the chicken breast in place of the extra sage leaves.

spatchcocked summer poussins

Serves **4**

Preparation time **30 minutes**,
  plus marinating

Cooking time **40 minutes**

grated zest and juice of
  2 lemons

7 tablespoons **olive oil**

4 **garlic cloves**, finely
  chopped

4 **poussins**, spatchcocked
  (see page 15)

small bunch **thyme**

4 **zucchini**, thickly sliced

2 **red onions**, cut into wedges

1 **red bell pepper**, cored,
  seeded, cut into chunks

1 **yellow bell pepper**, cored,
  seeded, cut into chunks

salt and **pepper**

Mix the lemon zest and juice with 4 tablespoons of the oil, the garlic, and seasoning. Put the poussins into a large shallow china dish, sprinkle with half the thyme stems, then spoon the lemon mixture over the top. Cover with plastic wrap and marinate in the refrigerator for 2 hours (or overnight if possible), turning once.

When ready to cook, thread 2 skewers crosswise through each poussin, from the thigh to the wing. Transfer to a large roasting pan and spoon over any marinade. Put all the vegetables into a separate roasting pan with the remaining oil and thyme stems and roast in a preheated oven, 375°F, for 40 minutes. Turn the vegetables, baste the chicken, and swop oven positions halfway through cooking until the chicken is browned and cooked when tested (see page 11). Transfer to serving plates and serve with warm ciabatta bread.

For soy spatchcocked poussins, mix the grated zest and juice of 1 lemon with the grated zest and juice of 1 lime, 2 tablespoons honey, 2 tablespoons dark soy sauce, and a 1½ inch piece of grated ginger root. Marinate and cook the poussins as above but without the vegetables, serving instead with salad and new potatoes.

chicken dinner for two

Serves **2**

Preparation time **20 minutes**

Cooking time **47 minutes**

13 oz **baking potatoes**,
   peeled, cut into chunks

1 tablespoon **olive oil**

13 oz **butternut squash**,
   peeled, seeded, cut into
   chunks

1 **parsnip**, peeled, cut into
   quarters

2 boneless, skinless **chicken
   breasts**, each about 5 oz

4 slices **bacon**

2 **bay leaves**

2 **garlic cloves**, halved

¾ cup **chicken stock**
   (see page 10)

salt and **pepper**

Add the potatoes to a saucepan of boiling water and cook for 5 minutes until just tender. Meanwhile, pour the oil into a roasting pan and place in a preheated oven, 400°F, for 5 minutes.

Drain the potatoes and shake in the colander to rough up their surfaces, then add to the hot oil with the squash and parsnip. Roast for 15 minutes.

Season the chicken breasts and wrap each with 2 slices of bacon. Turn the vegetables, then add the chicken, bay leaves, and garlic to the pan. Roast for 25 minutes until the vegetables are golden and the chicken cooked when tested (see page 11).

Transfer the chicken and vegetables to serving plates. Add the stock to the pan and bring to a boil, scraping up the pan juices. Season and boil for 2 minutes. Pour into a pitcher and serve with the chicken and vegetables.

For roast chicken with dauphinoise potatoes, prepare the chicken as above. Blanch 12 oz sliced potatoes in boiling water for 4 minutes. Drain and layer in a shallow ovenproof dish with ½ thinly sliced onion, 2 finely chopped garlic cloves, and seasoning. Pour over ⅔ cup heavy cream and dot with 1 tablespoon butter. Cook on the shelf above the chicken for 30 minutes until golden brown.

roast poussins with orange

Serves **4**
Preparation time **15 minutes**
Cooking time **50 minutes**

4 **poussins**
4 tablespoons **olive oil**
4 stems **rosemary**
1 large **orange**, cut into
   8 wedges
2 **red onions**, cut into wedges
½ cup **marinated green and**
   black olives
2 small **fennel bulbs**, thickly
   sliced
4 slices **Canadian bacon**
1¼ cups **chicken stock**
   (see page 10)
salt and **pepper**

Put the poussins into a large roasting pan, drizzle each with ½ tablespoon of oil, then sprinkle with seasoning and the leaves torn from the rosemary stems.

Squeeze the juice from the orange wedges over the top, then put a wedge inside each poussin, adding the rest to the roasting pan with the onion wedges, olives, and fennel.

Drape the bacon over the poussin breasts, pour the stock into the base of the roasting pan, and drizzle the remaining oil over the vegetables.

Roast in a preheated oven, 375°F, for 50 minutes, basting and turning the vegetables once during cooking until golden brown and the chicken cooked when tested (see page 11). Transfer to serving plates and serve with warm bread to mop up the pan juices.

For roast poussin with pimenton tomatoes, put the poussins into a roasting pan as above with the oil, seasoning, and rosemary. Add 2 red onions, cut into wedges, then 10 oz halved cherry tomatoes, 2 chopped garlic cloves, and ¼ teaspoon smoked paprika (pimenton) in place of the orange, olives, and fennel. Pour over 6 tablespoons red wine, 2 tablespoons balsamic vinegar, and some seasoning instead of the stock, and roast as above.

spatchcocked herb poussins

Serves **2**
Preparation time **10 minutes**
Cooking time **25–30 minutes**

2 **poussins**, spatchcocked
(see page 15)
1 tablespoon **olive oil**
chive flowers, to garnish
(optional)
salt and **pepper**

For the herb butter
¼ cup **butter**, softened
1 tablespoon chopped **chives**
1 tablespoon chopped **chervil**
or **parsley**
1 tablespoon chopped **fennel**
finely grated zest of ½ **lemon**
1 teaspoon **lemon juice**
salt and **pepper**

To make the herb butter, beat together the butter, chives, chervil or parsley, fennel, lemon zest and juice, salt, and plenty of pepper.

Season the poussins on both sides and brush them with the oil. Cook by broiling, chargrilling, or over the barbecue, turning them several times, until they are cooked through when tested (see page 11), which will take 25–30 minutes.

Transfer to serving plates, top with plenty of herb butter and sprinkle with chive flowers, if available.

For spatchcocked poussins with blue cheese & chili butter, mix ¼ cup butter with 2 oz crumbled blue cheese and ¼–½ mild red chili, seeded and finely chopped to taste. Prepare the poussins and continue as above.

two meals
from one

chicken & spinach chowder

Serves **6**
Preparation time **15 minutes**
Cooking time **35 minutes**

1 tablespoon **sunflower oil**
2 tablespoons **butter**
4 slices **Canadian bacon**,
  chopped
2 small **leeks**, thinly sliced,
  green and white slices
  separated
1½ lb **potatoes**, diced
3¾ cups **chicken stock**
  (see page 10)
5–7 oz **cooked chicken**,
  diced
1½ cups **lowfat milk**
⅔ cup **heavy cream**
2 cups **spinach**, rinsed,
  roughly chopped
nutmeg, grated
salt and **pepper**

Heat the oil and butter in a large saucepan, add the bacon, white leeks, and diced potatoes and cook over a low heat for 5 minutes, stirring until lightly golden.

Mix in the stock, then bring to a boil, cover, and simmer for 20 minutes until the potatoes are just tender. Add the chicken and boil rapidly for 3 minutes.

Stir in the green leeks, milk, cream, and a little salt and pepper. Simmer gently for 5 minutes, then stir in the spinach and a little nutmeg. Cook for 2 minutes until the spinach is just cooked.

Ladle into bowls, sprinkle with a little extra nutmeg, and serve with crusty bread.

For creamy chicken, bacon, & celeriac soup, use 1 chopped onion in place of the leeks and replace the potatoes with celeriac. Fry with the bacon as above. Roughly mash or puree the soup, then add the chicken and cook as above. Mix with cream and nutmeg but omit the spinach, adding 2 tablespoons chopped chives instead.

coconut chicken with noodles

Serves **4**
Preparation time **15 minutes**
Cooking time **20 minutes**

1 tablespoon **sunflower oil**
1 **onion**, finely chopped
1 inch piece **ginger root**,
  grated
2 **garlic cloves**, finely chopped
1 tablespoon **Thai red curry
  paste**
1¾ cups **light coconut milk**
⅔ cup **chicken stock**
  (see page 10)
3 teaspoons **fish sauce**
5–7 oz **cooked chicken**,
  torn into strips
10 oz pack fresh **stir-fry
  vegetables**
13 oz pack fresh **egg noodles**
small bunch **cilantro**

Heat the oil in a saucepan. Add the onion, ginger, and garlic and fry until pale golden. Stir in the curry paste, then mix in the coconut milk, chicken stock, and fish sauce.

Bring to a boil, stir in the chicken, cover, and simmer for 15 minutes. Stir in the vegetables and cook for 2 minutes, then add the noodles and the cilantro, torn into pieces, and heat until the noodles are piping hot.

Spoon into bowls and serve with chopsticks or a spoon and fork.

For coconut chicken with mixed greens, omit the noodles and ready-prepared stir-fry vegetables and use 5 cups mixed sliced bok choy, green beans, and broccoli instead. Cook for 4–5 minutes until just tender, then spoon into bowls and serve with rice.

chicken hotchpot

Serves **4**
Preparation time **15 minutes**
Cooking time **45 minutes**

1 tablespoon **sunflower oil**
1 **onion**, roughly chopped
2 small **potatoes**, diced
2 **carrots**, diced
2 small **parsnips**, diced
1 teaspoon **turmeric**
1 tablespoon **mild curry paste**
½ cup **red lentils**
5 cups **chicken stock**
  (see page 10)
3½–5 oz **cooked chicken**,
  diced
salt and **pepper**
small bunch **cilantro**,
  to garnish

Heat the oil in a saucepan, add the onion and fry, stirring, until pale golden. Mix in the remaining vegetables and fry for 2–3 minutes. Stir in the turmeric and curry paste, then add the lentils and stock.

Add the chicken and seasoning, then bring to a boil. Cover and simmer for 40 minutes, stirring occasionally, until the vegetables and lentils are softened.

Ladle into bowls and sprinkle with torn cilantro leaves. Serve with warm naan breads.

For chicken & barley broth, fry the onion as above, then add the potatoes, carrots, and just 1 parsnip, adding ¾ cup diced rutabaga as well. Omit the turmeric, curry paste, and red lentils and add ½ cup pearl barley. Add the stock and chicken as above, then season well, cover, and simmer for 1 hour until the barley is tender. Garnish with chopped parsley.

cheat's chicken & chorizo paella

Serves **4**
Preparation time **20 minutes**
Cooking time **25 minutes**

2 tablespoons **olive oil**
1 large **onion**, roughly chopped
5 oz **chorizo**, in one piece or
   sliced, peeled, diced
2 **garlic cloves**, finely chopped
1 **red bell pepper**, cored,
   seeded, diced
1 **orange bell pepper**, cored,
   seeded, diced
4 **tomatoes**, diced
1 cup **long-grain white rice**
large pinch **smoked paprika**
large pinch **saffron threads**
4–7 oz **cooked chicken**,
   diced
2½–3 cups **chicken stock**
   (see page 10)
⅔ cup **frozen peas**
½ cup **marinated mixed
   olives**
3 tablespoons chopped
   parsley (optional)

Heat the oil in a large skillet, add the onion and chorizo and fry, stirring, until the onion is pale golden. Stir in the garlic, peppers, and tomatoes and cook for 2–3 minutes until just softened.

Toss the rice in with the vegetables, then mix in the paprika, saffron, chicken, and about half the stock. Bring to a boil, stirring, then cover and simmer for about 20 minutes, topping up with remaining stock as needed.

Stir in the peas and olives and cook until the peas are cooked. Sprinkle with parsley, if desired, and spoon into bowls.

For chicken jambalaya, fry the onion in the oil with 5 oz chopped Canadian bacon. Add the garlic, peppers, and tomatoes, then mix in the rice. Flavor with 1 teaspoon Cajun spice instead of the paprika and saffron. Add the chicken and stock and simmer until tender. Omit the olives and add ⅔ cup sliced okra along with the peas at the end.

chicken & lentil pilaff

Serves **4**
Preparation time **15 minutes**
Cooking time **30–35 minutes**

1 tablespoon **olive oil**
1 **onion**, roughly chopped
2–3 **garlic cloves**, finely
  chopped
1 teaspoon **cumin seeds**,
  roughly crushed
2 teaspoons **coriander seeds**,
  roughly crushed
½ teaspoon **ground cinnamon**
13 oz can **chopped tomatoes**
2½–3 cups **chicken stock**
  (see page 10)
2 teaspoons **dark brown sugar**
½ cup **green lentils**
½ cup easy-cook **brown rice**
3½–5 oz **cooked chicken**,
  diced
small bunch **mint or cilantro**,
  torn, to garnish
½ cup **pistachio nuts**, halved,
  to garnish
salt and **pepper**

Heat the oil in the base of a saucepan, add the onion and fry until pale golden. Stir in the garlic and spices and cook for 1 minute, then mix in the tomatoes, 2½ cups of the stock, and sugar. Stir in the lentils, rice, chicken, and seasoning, and bring to a boil. Cover and simmer gently for 30–35 minutes until the rice and lentils are tender, topping up with the remaining stock as needed.

Spoon the pilaff into bowls, top with torn herbs, then sprinkle with the pistachios.

For chicken & bulghur pilaff, fry the onion and garlic in oil as above. Omit the cumin and coriander seeds, using ¼ teaspoon ground allspice instead with the cinnamon. Stir in the tomatoes, stock, sugar, and seasoning as above, then mix in 1 cup bulghur wheat, a 13½ oz can drained cranberry beans, and 3½–5 oz diced cooked chicken. Cover and simmer for 20 minutes. Garnish with lots of chopped parsley.

chicken & avocado salad

Serves **4**
Preparation time **15 minutes**

½ cup **light mayonnaise**
2 tablespoons **mango chutney**
grated zest and juice of **1 lime**
2 **avocados**, halved, pitted,
  peeled, diced
4 **scallions**, thinly sliced
¼ **cucumber**, diced
4–5 oz **cooked chicken**,
  diced
2 small **crisphead lettuces**
1 cup **mixed salad leaves**
small bunch **cilantro**, optional

Mix the mayonnaise, mango chutney, and lime zest together in a large bowl. Toss the lime juice with the avocados, then add to the dressing. Add the scallions, cucumber, and chicken and fold the mixture together lightly so that it is semi-mixed.

Divide the lettuce leaves between 4 serving plates and top with the other salad leaves. Spoon over the chicken salad and garnish with torn cilantro leaves, if desired. Serve immediately.

For chicken Waldorf salad, mix the same quantity of mayonnaise with the grated zest of ½ lemon, tossing the juice with 2 cored and diced dessert apples. Add the apples to the dressing along with ¼ cup golden raisins, 4 celery sticks, thickly sliced, and 4–5 oz diced cooked chicken. Serve on salad leaves as above, omitting the cilantro.

cheesy chicken & chutney puffs

Makes **9**
Preparation time **30 minutes**
Cooking time **20 minutes**

4 oz **cooked chicken**, diced
¼ cup diced **tomatoes**
⅛ cup **frozen corn**, defrosted
3 tablespoons **tomato chutney**
½ cup grated **mature cheddar cheese**
1 lb chilled **puff pastry**
flour, for rolling
1 **egg**, beaten

Mix the chicken, tomatoes, corn, and chutney together, then stir in two-thirds of the cheese.

Roll out half the pastry on a lightly floured surface and trim to a 12 inch square. Brush with the egg, then spoon the filling over the pastry in 9 evenly spaced mounds.

Roll out the remaining pastry until a little larger than the first layer, then place it over the other pastry square. Gently press down around the filling, then cut into 9 squares with a knife or pastry wheel. Transfer to an oiled baking sheet.

Brush the tops with a little more beaten egg, sprinkle with the remaining cheese, and bake in a preheated oven, 400°F, for 20 minutes until well risen and golden. Serve warm or cold with salad.

For cheesy chicken & spinach puffs, mix the cooked chicken with ½ cup low-fat cream cheese with garlic and herbs and ¾ cup frozen leaf spinach, defrosted and well drained. Season well with salt, pepper, and a little grated nutmeg. Dot the filling over the rolled-out pastry and continue as above.

curried chicken & couscous salad

Serves **4**
Preparation time **15 minutes**

1 cup **couscous**
⅓ cup **golden raisins**
2 teaspoons **mild curry paste**
1¾ cups **boiling water**
2 **tomatoes**, diced
½ **green, red,** or **yellow
  pepper**, cored, seeded,
  diced
½ **red onion**, finely chopped
small bunch **cilantro**, finely
  chopped
¾ cup lightly toasted
  shredded coconut
4–6 oz **cooked chicken**,
  diced
grated zest and juice of **1 lime**
3 tablespoons **sunflower oil**
salt and **pepper**

Put the couscous, golden raisins, and curry paste into
a large bowl, add the boiling water and mix together.
Allow to stand for 5 minutes.

Fluff up the couscous with a fork, then mix in the
tomatoes, pepper, onion, cilantro, coconut, and chicken.

Mix the lime zest and juice with the oil and a little
seasoning. Add to the couscous and toss together.
Spoon into bowls and serve.

For minted lemon couscous, omit the curry paste
and add 2 teaspoons harissa paste when soaking
the couscous and sultanas in boiling water. Stir in
½ green bell pepper, cored, seeded, and diced,
4 chopped scallions, ½ cup pistachio nuts, sliced,
and 3 tablespoons each chopped mint and parsley,
plus the chicken as above. Make up a dressing with
the grated zest and juice of ½ lemon, 3 tablespoons
olive oil, and seasoning.

mini chicken & broccoli frittatas

Makes **12**
Preparation time **15 minutes**
Cooking time **15 minutes**

8 oz **broccoli**, cut into small
  florets
oil, for greasing
4–5 oz **cooked chicken**,
  diced
6 **eggs**
½ cup **milk**
⅓ cup freshly grated
  Parmesan cheese
salt and **pepper**

Add the broccoli to a saucepan of boiling water and cook for 3 minutes, then drain into a colander. Brush the insides of a 12-section nonstick muffin pan with a little oil, then divide both the broccoli and the chicken between the sections.

Beat the eggs, milk, and Parmesan together in a pitcher, season generously, then pour the mixture over the broccoli and chicken.

Bake in a preheated oven, 375°F, for 15 minutes until well risen and golden. Loosen the edges of the frittatas, then turn out and serve with a tomato salad or baked beans.

For chicken, bacon, & red onion frittata, heat 1 tablespoon olive oil in a medium skillet, add 4 oz diced bacon and 1 sliced red onion and fry for 5 minutes until golden. Add 4–5 oz diced cooked chicken and fry until piping hot. Beat the eggs and milk together, then season. Add an extra 1 tablespoon oil to the pan, then pour in the egg mixture. Fry until the underside is golden, then finish off under a hot broiler until set and golden. Cut into wedges to serve.

index

5-spice powder: Asian
5-spice glazed chicken
110

aïoli: baked chicken with
aïoli 172
almonds
chicken skewers with
couscous 90
hot feta & almond
quinoa with seared
chicken 24
anchovies
chicken Caesar salad 42
warm chicken salad
with anchovies 42
apples
barbecued chicken with
apple slaw 46
chicken picnic terrine 58
chicken Waldorf salad
228
flamed chicken with
calvados & apple 148
maple glazed chicken
128
Normandy chicken 88
stoved chicken with
black pudding 120
apricots, dried
chicken skewers with
couscous 90
citrus chicken & fruited
bulghur 82
pickled walnut, apricot,
& chicken terrine 58
roast chicken with
apricot & walnut
stuffing 206
speedy spiced chicken
tagine 92
Asian citrus chicken
skewers 26
asparagus
griddled summer
chicken salad 44

roast chicken with
lemon baste 200
avocados
chicken & avocado
salad 228
chicken tacos & hot
green salsa 54
griddled chicken fajitas
62
guacamole 62
mojo chicken 76
mole toppings 154

baby leaf stir-fry with
chili 118
bacon
chicken & bacon thatch
132
chicken & spinach
chowder 218
chicken, bacon, & red
onion frittata 234
chicken, bacon, & sage
meatballs 130
chicken club sandwich
48
chicken dinner for two
210
chicken jambalaya 224
chicken Maryland with
fried bananas &
bacon 136
chicken picnic terrine
58
classic coq au vin 148
creamy chicken, bacon,
& celeriac soup 218
creamy chicken
gnocchi 114
pot-roast chicken with
vermouth 198
roast chicken with sage
& onion 206
roast poussins with
orange 212
stoved chicken with
bacon & sage 120
balsamic glazed chicken
110
baltis

chicken balti with
mushrooms &
spinach 126
chicken balti with whole
spices 126
bananas
chicken Maryland &
banana fritters 136
chicken Maryland with
fried bananas &
bacon 136
bean sprouts
Chinese cabbage &
bean sprout salad 106
gingered chicken with
bean sprout salad 20
black bean sauce: sesame
greens with black bean
sauce 102
black pudding: stoved
chicken with black
pudding 120
bok choy
coconut chicken with
mixed greens 220
lemon grass chicken &
vegetables 194
miso chicken broth 52
brandy
brandied chicken liver &
pistachio pâté 34
classic coq au vin 148
bread
chicken club sandwich
48
chicken liver toasts
60
chicken picnic loaf 68
chicken pitas with
carrot salad 38
chicken-liver crostini
142
curried chicken burgers
122
deli deluxe chicken
sandwich 48
griddled chicken
burgers 112
Italian pesto chicken
burgers 122

seared chicken
sandwich 22
tangy chicken, lemon,
and garlic toasties 22
Thai red chicken &
cashew sauce 36
broccoli
coconut chicken with
mixed greens 220
mini chicken & broccoli
frittatas 234
bulghur wheat
chicken & bulghur pilaff
226
citrus chicken & fruited
bulghur 82
burgers
curried chicken burgers
122
griddled chicken
burgers 112
Italian pesto chicken
burgers 122
Mediterranean burgers
112
butternut squash
chicken, butternut
squash, & sage risotto
114
chicken dinner for two
210
creamy chicken
gnocchi 114

calvados: flamed chicken
with calvados & apple
148
Caribbean chicken
skewers & salsa 138
Caribbean rice salad 138
cashew nuts: Thai red
chicken & cashew
sauce 36
Catalan chicken 88
celeriac: creamy chicken,
bacon, & celeriac soup
218
cheese
cheesy chicken &
chutney puffs 230

cheesy chicken & spinach puffs 230
cheesy fried chicken escalopes 178
chicken cacciatore 78
chicken club sandwich 48
chicken cordon bleu 190
chicken stacks 156
chicken with mozzarella & sundried tomatoes 94
chicken with spinach & ricotta 94
deli deluxe chicken sandwich 48
hot feta & almond quinoa with seared chicken 24
mole toppings 154
polenta crusted chicken strips 104
roast chicken with lemon baste 200
spatchcocked poussins with blue cheese & chili butter 214
Stilton-stuffed chicken with ham 190
chicken
  checking whether properly cooked 11
  how to carve a roast chicken 16–17
  how to joint a whole chicken 12–14
  how to spatchcock a chicken or poussin 15
  hygiene essentials 9
chicken stock 10
chicken tikka masala 124
chilies
  Asian chicken cakes 106
  baby leaf stir-fry with chili 118
  chicken salad with chili dressing 174
  chicken with chili and ginger jam 174

spatchcocked poussins with blue cheese & chili butter 214
sweet chili sauce 86
Chinese barbecued chicken wings 46
Chinese chicken wraps 56
Chinese cabbage
  Chinese cabbage & bean sprout salad 106
  teriyaki chicken with Asian salad 28
Chinese lemon chicken 182
chocolate: chicken mole 154
chorizo
  cheat's chicken & chorizo paella 224
  chicken caldo verde 72
  chicken with sweet potato wedges 30
cider
  cidered chicken puff pie 168
  pot-roast chicken with cider & mustard 198
coconut milk: coconut chicken with noodles 220
cognac: classic coq au vin 148
collard greens: sesame greens with black bean sauce 102
coq au vin, classic 148
corn
  cheesy chicken & chutney puffs 230
  chicken & bacon thatch 132
  chicken, frankfurter, & corn puff pie 168
coronation chicken 32
couscous
  chicken & pistachio couscous 68
  chicken skewers with couscous 90

curried chicken & couscous salad 232
griddled harissa chicken 166
minted lemon couscous 232
roasted chicken with herb couscous 90
speedy spiced chicken tagine 92
cranberries: chicken cushion with ginger & cranberries 184
cream: creamy chicken, bacon, & celeriac soup 218
curries
  curried chicken & couscous salad 232
  curried chicken burgers 122
  curried chicken with mixed vegetables 140
  Thai green chicken curry 170
  Thai red chicken curry 170
curry paste
  coronation chicken 32
  spiced chicken & mango salad 32

dates
chicken skewers with couscous 90
citrus chicken & fruited bulghur 82
citrus chicken salad 82
dumplings: chicken stew & dumplings 96

eggplants
curried chicken with mixed vegetables 140
peppered chicken & eggplants 140
tricolore stacks 156
eggs
  chicken, bacon, & red onion frittata 234

chicken bisteeya 186
chicken Caesar salad 42
egg fried rice 50
mini chicken & broccoli frittatas 234

fennel
chicken & fennel strogonoff 158
griddled chicken & fennel pockets 38
mixed roots with fennel & chicken 30
fettuccine: chicken cacciatore 78
frankfurters: chicken, frankfurter, & corn puff pie 168
frittatas
  chicken, bacon, & red onion frittata 234
  mini chicken & broccoli frittatas 234

galangal
Thai barbecued chicken 86
Thai red chicken curry 170
ginger
  Asian chicken cakes 106
  chicken cushion with ginger & cranberries 184
  chicken with chili and ginger jam 174
  gingered chicken with bean sprout salad 20
  gingered chicken with soft noodles 20
gnocchi: creamy chicken gnocchi 114
green Thai curry paste: Thai green chicken curry 170
guacamole
  citrus chicken wraps 76

griddled chicken fajitas 62
mojo chicken 76

ham
chicken cordon bleu 190
chicken stacks 156
chicken with spinach & ricotta 94
Stilton-stuffed chicken with ham 190
harissa
griddled harissa chicken 166
minted lemon couscous 232
Moroccan chicken & harissa 162
hoisin sauce
Chinese barbecued chicken wings 46
Chinese chicken wraps 56
honey: sticky chicken with honey & garlic 64
hummus: summer chicken wraps 44

Italian chicken cushion 184

jerk marinade: jerk chicken 40

kaffir lime leaves
Asian chicken cakes 106
lemon grass chicken & vegetables 194
Thai red chicken curry 170

lasagna: chicken & mushroom lasagna 164
leeks
chicken & spinach chowder 218
cidered chicken puff pie 168

lemon grass
Asian chicken cakes 106
lemon grass chicken & vegetables 194
stir-fried lemon grass chicken 194
Thai green chicken curry 170
lentils
chicken & barley broth 222
chicken & lentil pilaff 226
chicken hotchpot 222
chicken pimenton with puy lentils 80
chicken with sage & lemon 74
lemon-infused chicken with arugula & lentil salad 98
linguine: chicken cacciatore 78

macaroni: chicken arrabiata 84
mango chutney
chicken & avocado salad 228
chicken with pimento puree 192
mango chutney-glazed chicken 128
mangoes
mango chutney-glazed chicken 128
spiced chicken & mango salad 32
maple syrup: maple glazed chicken 128
marmalade: sticky marmalade chicken 100
mayonnaise
chicken & avocado salad 228
chicken Waldorf salad 228
coronation chicken 32

meatballs
chicken, bacon, & sage meatballs 130
chicken meatballs with mustard sauce 130
mini chicken meatballs with pimento puree 192
mint
minted lemon couscous 232
roasted chicken with herb couscous 90
mole toppings 154
Moroccan chicken & harissa 162
mushrooms
chicken and barley risotto 176
chicken & mushroom lasagna 164
chicken balti with mushrooms & spinach 126
chicken liver pâté with mushrooms 34
chicken risotto with wild mushrooms 188
hot & sour chicken soup 52
miso chicken broth 52
mustard
chicken meatballs with mustard sauce 130
deviled chicken 40
pot-roast chicken with cider & mustard 198
sticky mustard chicken & potatoes 100

nectarine chutney 146
noodles
chicken with chili and ginger jam 174
coconut chicken with noodles 220
gingered chicken with soft noodles 20
Normandy chicken 88

olives
chicken puttanesca 84
Mediterranean burgers 112
roast poussins with orange 212
oranges
chicken, tarragon, & orange salad 66
chicken, tarragon, & orange tagliatelle 66
Chinese barbecued chicken wings 46
citrus chicken & fruited bulghur 82
citrus chicken salad 82
jerk chicken 40
roast chicken with apricot & walnut stuffing 206
roast poussins with orange 212

pancetta: chicken liver & pancetta ragu 134
parsnips
chicken & barley broth 222
chicken dinner for two 210
chicken hotchpot 222
maple glazed chicken 128
mixed roots with fennel & chicken 30
roast chicken with spiced roots 204
pasta
creamy chicken rigatoni 80
penne with chicken livers 142
peanut butter
chicken with peanut sauce 50
Thai chicken satay 108
peanuts: chicken with peanut sauce 50
pearl barley
chicken & barley broth 222

chicken and barley
    risotto 176
penne with chicken livers
    142
Pernod: chicken & fennel
    strogonoff 158
pesto
    Italian pesto chicken
    burgers 122
    tricolore stacks 156
pilaffs
    chicken & bulghur pilaff
    226
    chicken & lentil pilaff
    226
pimenton
    chicken pimenton with
    puy lentils 80
    roast poussin with
    pimenton tomatoes
    212
pimentos
    chicken with pimento
    puree 192
    mini chicken meatballs
    with pimento puree
    192
pineapple
    blackened chicken &
    beans 116
    Caribbean chicken
    skewers & salsa
    138
piri piri chicken skewers
    26
pistachio nuts
    brandied chicken liver &
    pistachio pâté 34
    chicken & pistachio
    couscous 68
plums: Asian 5-spice
    glazed chicken 110
polenta crusted chicken
    strips 104
pomegranates: chicken
    liver & pomegranate
    salad 60
poussins
    how to spatchcock a
    poussin 15

roast poussin with
    pimenton tomatoes
    212
roast poussins with
    orange 212
soy spatchcocked
    poussins 208
spatchcocked herb
    poussins 214
spatchcocked poussins
    with blue cheese &
    chili butter 214
spatchcocked summer
    poussins 208

quinoa
hot feta & almond
    quinoa with seared
    chicken 24
quinoa salad with
    seared chicken 24

radishes: teriyaki
    chicken with Asian
    salad 28
ragus
    chicken & walnut ragu
    134
    chicken liver & pancetta
    ragu 134
red kidney beans: chicken
    mole 154
red Thai curry paste: Thai
    red chicken curry 170
rice
    blackened chicken with
    rice & peas 116
    Caribbean rice salad
    138
    cheat's chicken &
    chorizo paella 224
    chicken & lentil pilaff
    226
    chicken & red rice
    risotto 176
    chicken, butternut
    squash, & sage risotto
    114
    chicken risotto 188
    egg fried rice 50

risottos
    chicken and barley
    risotto 176
    chicken & red rice
    risotto 176
    chicken, butternut
    squash, & sage risotto
    114
    chicken risotto 188
    chicken risotto with wild
    mushrooms 188
rosemary: roast chicken
    with herbes de
    Provence 202

saffron chicken with
    mixed vegetables 180
salad leaves: chicken liver
    & pomegranate salad
    60
salads
    Caribbean rice salad
    138
    chicken & avocado
    salad 228
    chicken Caesar salad 42
    chicken liver &
    pomegranate salad 60
    chicken pitas with
    carrot salad 38
    chicken salad with chili
    dressing 174
    chicken, tarragon, &
    orange salad 66
    chicken Waldorf salad
    228
    Chinese cabbage &
    bean sprout salad 106
    citrus chicken salad 82
    curried chicken &
    couscous salad 232
    gingered chicken with
    bean sprout salad 20
    griddled summer
    chicken salad 44
    lemon-infused chicken
    with arugula & lentil
    salad 98
    pickled Thai cucumber
    salad 108

quinoa salad with
    seared chicken 24
roast chicken & white
    bean salad 78
spiced chicken &
    mango salad 32
spinach salad 162
teriyaki chicken with
    Asian salad 28
warm chicken salad with
    anchovies 42
salsas
    Caribbean chicken
    skewers & salsa 138
    chicken tacos & hot
    green salsa 54
    sweet potato jackets
    with chicken & tomato
    salsa 54
salt
    baked chicken in a salt
    crust 172
    salt & pepper chicken
    182
sandwiches
    club sandwich 48
    deli deluxe chicken
    sandwich 48
    seared chicken
    sandwich 22
satay: Thai chicken satay
    108
sauces
    chicken meatballs with
    mustard sauce 130
    chicken strips with
    garlicky tomato sauce
    104
    chicken with peanut
    sauce 50
    sweet chili sauce 86
    Thai red chicken &
    cashew sauce 36
sausages
    chicken cushion with
    ginger & cranberries
    184
    chicken picnic terrine 58
    Italian chicken cushion
    184

roast chicken with sage
& onion 206
sherried chicken
strogonoff 158
soups
chicken & barley broth
222
creamy chicken, bacon,
& celeriac soup 218
hot & sour chicken soup
52
miso chicken broth 52
soy spatchcocked
poussins 208
spaghetti
chicken puttanesca
84
lemon-infused chicken
& spaghetti 98
spices
barbecued spiced
chicken 204
roast chicken with spice
rub 202
roast chicken with
spiced roots 204
spinach
cheesy chicken &
spinach puffs 230
chicken & spinach
chowder 218
chicken balti with
mushrooms & spinach
126
chicken pimenton with
puy lentils 80

chicken with spinach &
ricotta 94
creamy chicken rigatoni
80
spinach salad 162
stews
chicken & vegetable
stew 92
chicken hotpot 96
chicken stew &
dumplings 96
Stilton-stuffed chicken
with ham 190
strogonoffs
chicken & fennel
strogonoff 158
sherried chicken
strogonoff 158
Szechuan chicken 102

Tabasco sauce: deviled
chicken 40
taco shells: chicken
tacos & hot green
salsa 54
tagines
chicken & tomato tagine
150
speedy spiced chicken
tagine 92
tagliatelle
chicken liver & pancetta
ragu 134
chicken, tarragon, &
orange tagliatelle
66

tandoori chicken, griddled
166
tandoori paste/powder:
griddled tandoori
chicken 166
tapenade: deli deluxe
chicken sandwich 48
teriyaki
teriyaki chicken with
Asian salad 28
teriyaki chicken with
three seeds 28
terrines
chicken picnic terrine 58
pickled walnut, apricot,
& chicken terrine 58
Thai barbecued chicken 86
Thai chicken satay 108
Thai green chicken curry
170
Thai red chicken &
cashew sauce 36
Thai red chicken curry 170
Thai red chicken with lime
-dressed zucchini 36
Thai sesame chicken
patties 118
thyme: roast chicken with
herbes de Provence
202
tomato chutney: cheesy
chicken & chutney puffs
230
tortillas
Chinese chicken wraps
56

citrus chicken wraps 76
griddled chicken fajitas
62
seared chicken &
vegetable wraps 56
summer chicken wraps
44

vermouth: pot-roast
chicken with vermouth
198

walnuts
chicken & walnut ragu
134
pickled walnut, apricot,
& chicken terrine 58
roast chicken with
apricot & walnut
stuffing 206
wine
chicken and barley
risotto 176
chicken & red rice
risotto 176
classic coq au vin 148

yogurt
coronation chicken 32
spiced chicken & mango
salad 32
spiced chicken with
yogurt crust 146

acknowledgments

Executive editor: Nicola Hill
Editor: Ruth Wiseall
Executive art editor: Sally Bond
Designer: Claire Dale for Cobalt Id
Photographer: David Munns
Home economist: Sara Lewis
Prop stylist: Liz Hippisley
Production controller: Carolin Stransky

Special photography: © Octopus Publishing Group
Limited/David Munns
Other photography: © Octopus Publishing Group
Limited.

The publisher would like to thank David Mellor
(4 Sloane Square, London SW1W 8EE, 0207 730
7240, www.davidmellordesign.co.uk) for the loan of
kitchen equipment, plates and cutlery.